dessert

recipes from
le champignon sauvage
david everitt-matthias

*As with my first book,
I dedicate this to my wife, Helen,
who provides me with more support
than I could possibly ask for.
Thank you so much.*

dessert

recipes from
le champignon sauvage
david everitt-matthias

foreword by
heston blumenthal

Absolute Press

First published in Great Britain
in 2009 by

Absolute Press
Scarborough House
29 James Street West
Bath BA1 2BT
Phone 44 (0) 1225 316013
Fax 44 (0) 1225 445836
E-mail info@absolutepress.co.uk
Website www.absolutepress.co.uk

Publisher
Jon Croft
Commissioning Editor
Meg Avent
Editor
Jane Middleton
Designer
Matt Inwood
Design Assistant
Claire Siggery
Indexer
Andrea O'Connor
Photographer
Lisa Barber
Photography Assistants
Hilary Knox and Neri Kamcili

A catalogue record of this book is
available from the British Library

ISBN 13: 9781906650032

Printed and bound by
Butler Tanner & Dennis,
Somerset

A note about the text
This book is set in Sabon MT.
Sabon was designed by Jan
Tschichold in 1964. The roman
design is based on type by Claude
Garamond, whereas the italic
design is based on types by Robert
Granjon.

Jacket image
Strawberry and hibiscus jelly with
lemon verbena custard and
blackcurrant sorbet (page 48)

contents

foreword by heston blumenthal

The world of cooking has changed in so many ways. We are now more exposed to other food cultures than ever before. Air travel, satellite television and the internet have expanded the culinary toolbox no end.

The growth of important international chefs' conferences where chefs demonstrate their techniques to the general public, their industry peers, colleagues and the worlds press, have meant that a whole new range of exciting techniques are now at the young chefs disposal.

There is however, a potential danger to all of this. It is incredibly important that chefs whilst embracing this new, exciting world, do not lose sight of the importance of the classical foundation of cooking – in essence the nuts and bolts needed to build a strong framework. Also, with the exciting potential of the wide range of exotic ingredients now available, it is more important than ever to champion and support local produce.

So, how does this relate to David?

Dedication to his craft and an impressive list of achievements has established David as one of the very best British chefs ever to cook in this country. He is a shining light to professional and amateur cooks alike.

David will embrace technology, but never let it get in the way of his craft. He respects tradition, but will move things on when he feels that there are genuine improvements to be made.

He has been quietly foraging and championing not only British but local British produce for years.

All in all, David Everitt-Matthias is the epitome of what a truly great modern day chef should be and in this book he shares his creativity, knowledge for his craft, techniques and diverse use of produce, some of which might even be lurking at the end of your garden!

This is an exciting, informative and truly delicious book.

Heston Blumenthal
Bray, February 2009

introduction

I so enjoy finishing a meal with a good dessert. It just isn't complete without one. Whether it's a light summer dessert or a heavier, more comforting winter pud, the most important thing is that it should be full of flavour, as palates can flag towards the end of a meal.

I find desserts immensely rewarding to create, particularly as you can take more time with the composition and presentation than with other parts of the meal. Yet I didn't train as a pastry chef and have largely had to teach myself. When I started my career at the Inn on the Park, in London, I spent five happy years covering vegetables, roasts and grills, sauces, fish and the larder section but, as in so many large restaurant kitchens, the pastry section remained elusive. It was quite separate from the rest of the kitchen and was not considered part of a chef's apprenticeship.

Much later, when I opened Le Champignon Sauvage, I was very conscious of the gap in my knowledge. There was only myself and one other person working here to begin with, so the two of us had to cover every area of the kitchen. It was from this point that my learning began.

I read books and experimented endlessly. I had no preconceptions, so the more I found out, the more I began to ask questions: what would happen if I used a different flour for this, a different sugar for that, what would happen if I added things, subtracted things? I applied the same logic to desserts as I did to the rest of my cooking. As the years progressed, my knowledge about ingredients increased, and I now draw upon a much more varied larder. My desserts repertoire has opened up with wild foods, spices and even vegetables. Twenty-two years after Le Champignon Sauvage opened, I still get a real buzz from bringing new flavours to the dessert table, and experimenting with ingredients such as Jerusalem artichokes, white asparagus and sorrel, pandan leaves, green tea and gorse flowers.

In 1996 our efforts were rewarded when I was named Dessert Chef of the Year in a competition run by the Egon Ronay Guide – an award I was honoured to receive, as there were still only the two of us in the kitchen and we had beaten some of the top Michelin-starred restaurants with their own pastry departments. Now I have a bigger brigade, but I still don't employ a pastry chef. Instead, the chefs who work here go through the pastry section along with all the others, so they can turn their hand to any part of the kitchen. I believe it is very important that the head chef's style and palate are in evidence from the starters and main courses right through to dessert and petits fours. Otherwise, there will be a break in the continuity of the meal.

David Everitt-Matthias
Cheltenham, February 2009

'I read books and experimented endlessly. I had no preconceptions, so the more I found out, the more I began to ask questions: what would happen if I used a different flour for this, a different sugar for that, what would happen if I added things, subtracted things? I applied the same logic to desserts as I did to the rest of my cooking.'

how to use my book

As in my previous book, Essence *(Absolute Press, 2006), most of the dishes are made up of several separate components, each of which has its own heading in the ingredients list and the method. That way, if you want to skip a particular element in a recipe, or prepare parts of it a day or two in advance, it is very easy to do. Desserts lend themselves remarkably well to this relaxed style of cooking.*

Remember, a first-rate dessert needs first-rate ingredients. Always use the freshest ingredients you can find. If you go for inferior ones, the taste and texture just won't be there.

Getting hold of good food doesn't have to be expensive. In the soft fruit season, there are many pick-your-own farms that are a joy to visit, providing the freshest possible fruit and frequently offering very good value. There are also berries, blossoms, herbs, nuts, apples and plums available in the wild, so keep your eyes open on a countryside ramble – you never know what you might find.

In the introductions to the recipes, I have encouraged you to use your imagination and try substituting different ingredients. This is how many chefs come up with new creations and, as long as you think logically about flavour combinations, it is a wonderful way to extend your repertoire. Don't forget you can also vary ingredients such as sugars to give a different flavour or texture. Cooking should be fun and creative, so do play around and, above all, enjoy yourself.

All the measurements in this book are in metric, since precision is very important when making desserts. It is worth investing in a good set of scales that will measure accurately down to the last gram. Liquids are given in millilitres, as is usual for the domestic kitchen. In the restaurant, however, I prefer to measure liquids in grams, which is easily done with digital scales. Millilitres and grams are interchangeable when it comes to liquids.

a note on ingredients

butter
I prefer to use unsalted butter, as it enables you to be more precise when it comes to seasoning. I buy my butter from a small dairy in Stow-on-the-Wold.

lecithin
Lecithin is invaluable for helping foams become more stable. I get it from my local healthfood shop in the form of soya lecithin granules, which I then grind to a powder in a spice mill. It can be stored like this and used when needed.

chocolate
For this book I have for the most part used the two types of chocolate that are most readily obtainable: 64 and 71 per cent cocoa solids.

measurements
Finally, I have given liquid measures in millilitres throughout this book, as most domestic cooks are more accustomed to working in this way. However, I prefer to measure liquids in grams, which is easily done with a set of digital scales. Millilitres and grams are interchangeable when it comes to liquids.

Clockwise from top-left: Adam Brown; Gary Pearce; Ciaran Sweeney; me.

14 *dessert* *introduction*

Clockwise from top-left: Justyna Juszczuk; Perrine Junalik; Stephanie Ronssin; Helen.

foundations

Here are some of the things we keep on hand to add to our desserts, plus a few basics such as sweet pastry and brioche. They are used regularly throughout the book and can be adapted to suit your own recipes.

marinated prunes in armagnac

These prunes are so addictive, and so easy to prepare. You can experiment with many different spices and flavourings, juices, wines and spirits to enliven them. For me, the best way to eat marinated prunes is with warm rice pudding with lots of fresh vanilla in it. It reminds me of schooldays, but much better, of course.

1 orange
1 lemon
750ml water
200g caster sugar
1 vanilla pod
1 cinnamon stick

1kg agen prunes
3 English Breakfast tea bags
250ml Armagnac

Peel the zest off the orange and lemon in long strips, then squeeze out the juice. Place the zest and juice, water, sugar, vanilla and cinnamon in a pan large enough to hold the prunes and bring to the boil, stirring to dissolve the sugar.

Simmer for 5 minutes, then add the prunes and place the tea bags on top. Remove from the heat and leave to macerate overnight.

The next day, remove the tea bags from the mixture and pour in the Armagnac. Mix carefully to distribute the Armagnac evenly. Store in a Kilner jar for 1 month before use – if you can wait!

white port and verjus syrup

Just as simple to make as the Maury Syrup, opposite, this has a fresh sweet and sour flavour. It was once made with tart crab apples but these days verjus (sour grape juice) is more popular. It's very good with white chocolate, peaches, apricots and grapes. For a more honeyed taste, try mead instead of white port.

2 bottles of white port
1 litre verjus
25g Demerara sugar

Place all the ingredients in a heavy-based pan and bring to the boil. Simmer slowly until reduced to 300ml, then strain through a fine sieve and leave to cool. Keep in a small squeezy bottle, ready for use.

maury syrup

Maury wine comes from the Roussillon area of France and is available as red and a lesser known white. The red is powerful and sweet, with a good hint of plums and caramelised raisins.

This syrup will keep for a very long time. Just store it in a small bottle in the fridge and it is ready to use. It has a wonderful deep flavour that goes well with warm spices, such as cinnamon and cloves. It is also a perfect match for figs, chocolate and citrus, so you see it is a bit of an all-rounder, and well worth making.

2 bottles of red Maury wine
1 bottle of red wine, such as a Rhône
a small handful of golden raisins
25g Demerara sugar

Place all the ingredients in a heavy-based pan and bring to the boil. Simmer slowly until reduced to 275ml, then strain through a fine sieve and leave to cool. Keep in a small squeezy bottle, ready for use.

orange powder

This is a must for the store cupboard. It makes a great finish for a dessert – sprinkled on top of a parfait, for example, or mixed with a little craquant to rest an ice cream or sorbet on. You can also use it to flavour ice cream or add it to the pan when sautéing fruit. It goes particularly well with liquorice, ginger and burdock and can give a zing to anything. Why not try it with lemon or lime instead?

4 large oranges
100g granulated sugar
250ml water

Remove the zest from the oranges with a vegetable peeler, trying to avoid the white pith. Place the sugar and water in a saucepan and bring to the boil, stirring to dissolve the sugar. Simmer for 2 minutes, then add the orange zest and cook gently for 15 minutes. Remove from the heat and leave to cool.

Drain off the excess syrup and scatter the strips of orange zest over a large baking sheet lined with baking parchment, making sure they aren't touching each other. Place in an oven preheated to 120°C/Gas Mark $1/2$ and leave for $1-1^1/_2$ hours, until completely dry; they should not be coloured at all. Leave to cool, then grind to a powder in a spice grinder. Store in a sealed jar in a cupboard; it will keep for 1 month.

salted lemons

These lemons are quick and easy to prepare, although they do have to be kept for a while to soften before use. Popular in Moroccan cooking, they have a very long shelf life and add so much flavour and freshness to dishes. Although they are commonly used in savoury cooking, they are great with chocolate, both bitter and white, acting as a foil to cut the richness. You could include a few stalks of lemongrass or a few lime leaves with them. Why not replace the lemons with oranges or limes and add some crushed coriander seeds and cardamom pods?

12 lemons, cut lengthways into quarters,
*   but not quite all the way through*
250g coarse sea salt
2 bay leaves
200ml lemon juice
about 200ml olive oil

Sprinkle the inside of the lemons with the salt and pack a third of them into a large, wide-necked jar. Add the bay leaves and sprinkle with a little more salt. Push down well to release the juices. Repeat with another third of the lemons, pushing down well. Add the final third and pour in the lemon juice. The lemons should be well covered with juice. If necessary, add enough olive oil to cover; this will form a seal that the air cannot penetrate. Wipe the neck of the jar clean and seal. Leave for at least 1 month before use, so the peel will soften. The juice can be used, as can the pulp. To use the peel, just quickly rinse under cold running water first.

cardamom yoghurt

Of course, you don't have to make your own yoghurt, but we do at the restaurant. It takes so little time and you can be sure of injecting your own personal taste into it. You can create so many flavours: coriander, vanilla, coffee, liquorice, oh I could go on and on. But one of my favourites just has to be cardamom. The slight acidity of the yoghurt and the almost citrus tang of the cardamom just seem to be made for each other. I use it for adding a light touch to desserts. It can help cut the richness of chocolate and is a great accompaniment to anything citrus. So a small yoghurt maker is essential in our kitchen. If you want to make plain yoghurt, just omit the cardamom from this recipe.

10 cardamom pods
1 litre whole milk
200g natural live yoghurt

Place the cardamom and milk in a saucepan and bring to the boil. Remove from the heat and cool down to 35°C. Pass through a fine sieve, then mix in the live yoghurt and place in a yoghurt maker. Leave for 8–10 hours, then store in the fridge until needed.

If you want a thicker yoghurt, add 35g of dried skimmed milk powder to the milk before boiling. After the initial use of bought live yoghurt, you can use 200g of your own homemade yoghurt for the next batch.

sweet pastry

I devised this sweet pastry when I was in the National Chef of the Year competition and wanted something that would be very quick to prepare and wouldn't shrink if it was cooked without resting first.

Ground pistachios or walnuts could be used instead of almonds, or you could substitute Demerara sugar for icing sugar to give a completely different taste.

270g plain flour
150g cold unsalted butter
50g ground almonds
grated zest of 1 lemon or 1 orange
seeds from 1 vanilla pod
100g icing sugar
1 egg
1 egg yolk

Place all the ingredients except the egg and egg yolk in a food processor and pulse until the mixture resembles breadcrumbs. Add the egg and yolk and pulse until the mixture starts to form a ball. Turn out on to a floured surface and knead as lightly as possible, just until smooth. Form into a ball, flatten, then wrap in cling film and chill for at least 3 hours before use. This pastry is suitable for freezing; thaw for 24 hours in the fridge.

puff pastry

Puff pastry is one of those things that takes ages to make but is always so rewarding when finished and you are eating the feather-light results. You could add lemon and orange zest to it to use with raspberries and strawberries, or add a little cinnamon or ground ginger. Alternatively, try including some ground wattleseeds or roasted acorns, or simply replace a little of the flour with bitter cocoa powder to make chocolate puff pastry.

500g strong white flour
1¹/₂ teaspoons salt
550g unsalted butter
1 teaspoon lemon juice or white wine vinegar
320ml ice-cold water

Sift the flour and salt into a bowl. Dice 100g of the butter, add to the flour and rub it in until the mixture resembles breadcrumbs. Add the lemon juice or vinegar to the water and gradually stir into the flour and butter until the mixture forms a smooth ball. Wrap in cling film and place in the fridge to relax for 30 minutes.

Soften the remaining butter by putting it between 2 sheets of cling film and hitting it with a rolling pin, being careful not to tear the cling film. Turn it over and repeat. Push the butter back into the centre of the cling film and repeat once more. Take the pastry out of the fridge and unwrap it. The pastry and butter should be the same temperature.

Roll the dough out to a 20 x 30cm rectangle. Roll out the butter, still wrapped in the cling film, to 15 x 25cm. Unwrap the butter, place it on one half of the pastry and fold the other half over, pressing the edges together well to seal in the butter. Now think of your pastry as a book and turn the dough so you have the spine to the left and the pages to the right. Roll out to 3 times its original size. One of the keys to the success of a good puff pastry is that the corners and edges must be level and neat at all times, so if they are not, lightly stretch the pastry to shape and try to keep this perfect rectangle.

Fold the dough into 3, keeping the edges neat. Place in the fridge for 30 minutes to relax. Then roll out a second time, keeping the spine to the left and pages to the right. Fold into 3 again, making sure that the edges are in line and neat. Return to the fridge for 30 minutes. Remove from the fridge and repeat the rolling process for a third time. Wrap and place back in the fridge until needed.

brioche

Wonderfully light and rich, brioche has all sorts of uses in desserts, either whole or in crumbs. It's also very good made into French toast, which I then like to top with a thin slice of marzipan and flash under the grill for a sort of sweet Welsh rarebit.

Makes 2 loaves

50ml warm water
20g fresh yeast
40g caster sugar
500g strong white flour
5 eggs, whisked and strained through a sieve
10g salt
300g unsalted butter, softened and diced
a little milk for brushing

Put the warm water in a small bowl and mix in the yeast and sugar until dissolved. Leave for 2–3 minutes, until frothy. Place the flour in an electric mixer and add the yeast mix. Slowly pour in the eggs and beat for 2 minutes on a low speed, adding the salt with the eggs. Add the butter bit by bit, waiting until each piece has been incorporated before adding the next.

Divide the mixture in half. Butter 2 loaf tins and line the bases with baking parchment. Put the dough in the tins, cover with a damp cloth and leave to prove at fairly warm room temperature (26°C) for 45–60 minutes, until doubled in size.

Lightly brush the top of the loaves with a little milk and place in an oven preheated to 180°C/Gas Mark 4. Bake for 45 minutes, until the brioche is golden and sounds hollow when tapped underneath. Leave to cool in the tins for 5 minutes, then turn out on to a wire rack and leave to cool completely. You could keep one loaf in the freezer if it is to be used for toast, as long as it is well wrapped.

spiced bread

Spiced bread is very versatile and can be served with afternoon tea or used to flavour ice creams, parfaits and mousses. It makes great French toast and goes perfectly with roasted apples and pears.

Made into breadcrumbs and then dried in the oven, it adds texture to a dish – sprinkled on top of a parfait for example. Diced and fried, it provides a contrasting texture for poached fruits such as cherries.

100ml milk
200g chestnut honey
150g rye flour
150g plain white flour
75g Demerara sugar
25g baking powder
75g unsalted butter, diced
2 eggs
grated zest of 1 orange
grated zest of 1/2 lemon
50g candied orange peel, finely diced (optional)
50g candied angelica, finely diced (optional)
5g ground ginger
5g ground green aniseed
3g ground cinnamon
2g ground nutmeg
1g ground cloves

Warm the milk and dissolve the honey in it, then leave to cool.

Place both the flours, the Demerara sugar, baking powder and diced butter in the bowl of an electric mixer. Mix on a low speed until the texture resembles breadcrumbs, then add the eggs and the honey mixture and beat until smooth. Add all the remaining ingredients and mix well. Pour into a greased lined loaf tin, about 20 x 7.5 x 7.5cm. Bake in an oven preheated to 160°C/Gas Mark 3 for 45–50 minutes, until deep golden and firm to the touch. Leave to cool in the tin for 20 minutes, then turn out on to a wire rack to cool completely.

chocolate and nut

I just had to give these two ingredients a chapter to themselves. They are eternally popular and there are myriad possibilities for using them. As a combination, they were made for each other.

The flavour of chocolate is normally determined by the amount of cocoa mass, or cocoa solids, in it. The popular confectionery that we eat in the form of bars, sweets, Easter eggs, etc., tends to contain a lower proportion of this mass, and therefore less chocolate. The higher you go up the mass ladder, the more chocolate and less sugar is used, until you get to 100 per cent cocoa mass, which is very savoury indeed. When we have a new member of staff at the restaurant, we get them to taste all the varieties and percentages of chocolate that we happen to have in and very few like the 100 per cent. For this book I have used mainly the two that are most readily obtainable: 64 and 71 per cent cocoa solids.

All good chocolate has its own characteristics: some are from single estates, like wine, and have floral, fruity and spicy tones, even tobacco notes. I love to add powerful flavours to it; after all, with something as rich and complex as this, there is no point being fainthearted. So many flavourings work with chocolate – from herbs such as rosemary, lavender, thyme, bay and verbena to spices like star anise, cinnamon, coriander, cardamom, liquorice and even cumin, plus oddities such as chilli, tobacco and beetroot. These all stand up to the chocolate and play with your palate. A tip for melting chocolate in a microwave: I have found that if you chop it up, place a third of it in the microwave and melt it completely, then add the remaining two-thirds, put it back in the microwave for 30 seconds, remove it and stir until melted, it will come out beautifully shiny.

Nuts make wonderful desserts. They all have their own unique flavour and texture, which can be changed by roasting or caramelising. When ground, they can be used to make frangipane and cakes; left a little coarser, they work well in pastries such as baklavas. They can be used fresh and young – early almonds, for example with their creamy taste and texture, are perfect with a late-summer fruit soup or delicate white peaches. Strong, bitter nuts such as walnuts go well with all the autumnal fruits. When composing a dish, it is worth playing around with ground nuts – substituting pistachios or walnuts for almonds, for example – to create a different effect.

'So many flavourings work with chocolate – from herbs such as rosemary, lavender, thyme, bay and verbena to spices like star anise, cinnamon, coriander, cardamom, liquorice and even cumin, plus oddities such as chilli, tobacco and beetroot.'

'Nuts make wonderful desserts. They all have their own unique flavour and texture, which can be changed by roasting or caramelising.'

chocolate yoghurt with prune purée

The sweet and sour taste of the prune purée makes it a perfect partner for chocolate, while the lactic acid in the yoghurt helps cut the richness, creating a lighter dessert. If you want something a little richer, simply double the amount of chocolate. You could replace the prune purée with a banana one and the chocolate with thick caramel. You could also consider flavouring the yoghurt with different spices, but I do like to use cardamom in this dessert.

If you have problems finding the grue de cacoa, just grate a little of the bitterest chocolate you can find on top. It won't have the same crunch but it will taste fine.

Serves 8 as a pre-dessert

for the chocolate yoghurt
100g bitter chocolate (64 per cent cocoa solids), chopped
1 quantity of Cardamom Yoghurt (see page 18)

for the prune purée
250g Marinated Prunes in Armagnac (see page 16), plus 75ml of their liquid

to serve
50g grue de cacao, roughly ground

chocolate yoghurt
Place the chopped chocolate in a bowl and melt over a pan of simmering water or in a microwave (see page 23). Divide the cardamom yoghurt in half and pour one portion on to the warm melted chocolate, whisking all the time. Set aside at room temperature until needed. Keep the remaining cardamom yoghurt in the fridge.

prune purée
Remove the stones from the prunes. Place the prunes in a liquidiser with the liquid and blend until smooth.

serving
Layer some of the chocolate yoghurt, prune purée and cardamom yoghurt in 8 glasses. Repeat until the glasses are almost full. Sprinkle over the grue de cacao. You can, if you wish, keep them in the fridge at this stage until needed. Just remove from the fridge 20 minutes before serving.

pistachio and dried apricot tart

This is one of my favourite tarts. In the restaurant, we use the very green Sicilian pistachios, which cost a little more but the flavour and colour are so much better. Walnuts, macadamia nuts and almonds would also work well, and the walnut version is particularly good made with dried figs.

You could use fresh apricots in the tart but I prefer the slight caramel flavour of dried ones, where the job of removing any excess water has already been done. Great with Pistachio Ice Cream (see page 31) or an apricot sorbet or even both.

Serves 10–12

for the pistachio frangipane
375g unsalted butter
375g caster sugar
180g plain flour
90g ground almonds
285g green pistachios, ground
6 eggs

for the tart
1 quantity of Sweet Pastry (see page 19)
750g dried apricots
100ml apricot brandy
125g caster sugar
300ml water
1 vanilla pod, split open lengthwise
100g pistachios, chopped
icing sugar for dusting

pistachio frangipane
Cream the butter and sugar together until pale and fluffy. Sift the flour, ground almonds and pistachios into a bowl. In a separate bowl, beat the eggs until pale. Add a little egg to the butter mixture, beating all the time, then a little of the flour mixture. Repeat until all the flour and eggs have been used. The mixture should be light, creamy and smooth. Keep in a cool place until needed.

tart
Roll out the pastry on a lightly floured work surface and use to line a buttered loose-bottomed tart tin, 22cm in diameter and 3–3.5cm deep. Chill for 40–50 minutes, then prick the base with a fork. Line the pastry case with baking parchment and fill with rice or baking beans. Place on a baking sheet in an oven preheated to 180°C/Gas Mark 4 and bake blind for 10–15 minutes, until very lightly coloured. Carefully remove the paper and beans and return the pastry case to the oven for 1–2 minutes to dry out a little.

Place the apricots, apricot brandy, caster sugar, water and vanilla pod in a saucepan and bring to the boil, stirring to dissolve the sugar. Turn the heat down to a simmer and cook gently for 10 minutes. Remove from the heat and put aside for a couple of hours so the apricots plump up.

Place a quarter of the apricots in a liquidiser and blend to a smooth purée, using a little of the cooking syrup to thin it down. The consistency should be like soft butter. Spread this mixture evenly over the base of the pastry case; it will make a very thin layer. Next add a third of the pistachio frangipane and spread it evenly over the apricot purée. Place the tart in the fridge until the filling has firmed up, then arrange the soaked apricots carefully on top. Cover with the remaining frangipane, smoothing the surface with a palette knife.

Sprinkle with the chopped pistachios and place in an oven preheated to 160°C/Gas Mark 3. Bake for 40–50 minutes, until the top is golden and a knife inserted in the centre comes out clean. Leave to rest for 15 minutes.

serving
Carefully unmould the tart and dust it with icing sugar. Cut into 10–12 slices and serve. Any leftovers are great the next day, chilled or warmed through.

pink praline tart with white chocolate sorbet

Pink pralines are almonds with a knobbly pink candy coating. They are available from MSK (see page 148), who will also supply the invert sugar paste needed for the white chocolate sorbet. The first time I had pink pralines was as a dainty petit four on one of my frequent visits to a restaurant in Rouen called Gill – a wonderful establishment that goes from strength to strength.

This is quite a rich dessert, hence the smaller tart base. I have paired it with white chocolate sorbet here because the flavours are very complementary. You could, however, replace the sorbet with toasted almond ice cream or even Roasted Banana Ice Cream (see page 77).

Serves 8

for the white chocolate sorbet
300g white chocolate, chopped
500ml water
125g Trimoline (invert sugar paste)
200ml milk
35g caster sugar
juice of 1/4 lemon

for the pink praline tart
1/2 quantity of Sweet Pastry (see page 19)
450g pink pralines
400ml double cream
50g unsalted butter

for the caramelised almonds
200g caster sugar
50ml water
200g blanched almonds
a pinch of salt
25g unsalted butter

white chocolate sorbet
Place the chopped chocolate in a bowl. Put the water, sugar paste, milk and sugar in a saucepan, bring to the boil and simmer for 1 minute. Leave to cool for about 3 minutes, then pour the mixture over the white chocolate and stir until dissolved.

Add the lemon juice and mix well. Push the mixture through a fine sieve and then freeze in an ice-cream machine according to the manufacturer's instructions. Transfer to the fridge to soften slightly about 10 minutes before serving.

pink praline tart
Roll out the pastry on a lightly floured surface and use to line a buttered loose-bottomed tart tin, 20cm in diameter and 3cm deep. Chill for 40–50 minutes. Prick the base all over with a fork, line with a sheet of baking parchment and fill with rice or baking beans. Place on a baking sheet in an oven preheated to 180°C/Gas Mark 4 and bake blind for 10–15 minutes, until the pastry is dry and lightly coloured. Carefully remove the paper and beans and set the pastry case to one side.

Crush the pink pralines into small pieces with the end of a rolling pin. Place them in a heavy-based saucepan with the double cream and butter and bring to the boil.

Cook, stirring from time to time, until the mixture reaches 145°C on a sugar thermometer; stir it more frequently as it nears the required temperature. Remove from the heat and pour into the prepared pastry case. Place the tart in the oven at 150°C/Gas Mark 2 and bake for 20 minutes. Carefully remove from the oven and leave to cool. Refrigerate until needed.

caramelised almonds
Place the sugar and water in a heavy-based pan and bring slowly to the boil, stirring to dissolve the sugar. Raise the heat and cook, without stirring, until the mixture turns into a deep golden caramel. Remove the pan from the heat, add the almonds, salt and butter and stir until all the nuts are coated in the caramel and the butter has melted. As the mixture cools down, the nuts will start to be individually coated. Tip on to a lightly oiled baking tray and leave to cool completely, pushing the mixture around a little to separate the nuts. Store in an airtight jar.

serving
Using a knife dipped in hot water, cut the tart into 8 slices. Serve topped with a scoop of white chocolate sorbet and some of the caramelised almonds.

hazelnut cake with pistachio ice cream and toasted almond cream

This dessert combines three of the best-known nuts. You could, however, swap them for cashews, macadamias and brazils for a rather different taste. Dried and fresh fruits go very well with nuts, so you could add some diced figs to the cake, if you like, or perhaps serve it with a peach cream to replace the almond cream – there are so many combinations to choose from.

Serves 8–10

for the pistachio ice cream
200g very green Sicilian pistachios
300ml milk
7g milk powder
200ml double cream
6 egg yolks
60g caster sugar
10ml liquid glucose

for the toasted almond cream
700ml double cream
100ml milk
75g toasted sliced almonds
110g caster sugar
3 gelatine leaves

for the hazelnut cake
225g hazelnuts, ground
50g plain flour
1 teaspoon baking powder
3 eggs
200g caster sugar
200g unsalted butter, melted and cooled
juice of 1 lemon
icing sugar for dusting (optional)

for the caramelised hazelnuts
200g caster sugar
50ml water
24 hazelnuts, toasted and skinned

to serve
25g pistachio nuts

pistachio ice cream

Spread the pistachios out on a baking sheet and toast them very lightly in an oven preheated to 160°C/Gas Mark 3 without letting them colour, just to release the oils a little.

Put the milk, milk powder and cream in a heavy-based saucepan and bring slowly to the boil. Remove from the heat, add the pistachios, then pour into a liquidiser and blend until smooth. Return the mixture to the saucepan and slowly bring to the boil again. Meanwhile, whisk the egg yolks, caster sugar and glucose together in a bowl.

Pour half the milk mixture on to the egg yolks, whisking constantly, then return it to the pan. Cook over a low heat, stirring continuously with a wooden spoon, until the mixture has thickened enough to coat the back of the spoon (it should register about 84°C on a thermometer). Strain immediately through a fine sieve into a bowl and leave to cool. Freeze in an ice-cream machine according to the manufacturer's instructions. Transfer to the fridge to soften slightly about 10 minutes before serving.

toasted almond cream

Put the cream, milk, toasted almonds and sugar in a heavy-based pan and bring gently to the boil. Pull to the side of the stove and leave to infuse for 40 minutes to extract as much of the almond flavour as possible.

Soak the gelatine in cold water for about 5 minutes, until soft and pliable, then squeeze out all the water. Bring the almond mixture back to the boil, then remove from the heat and add the gelatine, whisking until dissolved. Strain the mixture through a fine sieve, pressing on the almonds to extract as much juice as you can. Leave to cool, then pour into 8–10 lightly oiled dariole moulds, about 100ml in capacity. Cover and place in the fridge for at least 4 hours, until set.

hazelnut cake

Mix the ground hazelnuts, flour and baking powder together and set aside. Whisk the eggs and caster sugar together until pale, then slowly whisk in the melted butter. Fold in the hazelnut mixture, followed by the lemon juice. Transfer to a buttered lined round 23cm springform cake tin and place in an oven preheated to 160°C/Gas Mark 3. Bake for 40 minutes; the cake should still be slightly underdone in the middle so the cooling process will finish it off. Allow to cool in the tin for 10 minutes, then turn out on to a wire rack to cool completely. Dust with icing sugar, if using.

caramelised hazelnuts

Place the sugar and water in a thick-bottomed pan and heat gently, stirring to dissolve the sugar. Raise the heat, bring to the boil and cook without stirring until the syrup turns into a deep golden caramel. Immediately remove the pan from the heat, add the hazelnuts and stir until they are coated in the caramel. As the mixture cools down, the nuts will start to be individually coated. Tip the mixture on to a lightly oiled baking tray and pull the hazelnuts away from the others one at a time, creating a long tail of caramel behind each nut. Be careful, as they will be very hot; using a skewer to pierce the nut might help. Line them up on a tray carefully – they will be very brittle – and leave to cool

serving

Cut the cake into 8–10 slices and place on serving dishes. Dip the almond cream moulds in some hot water for 2–3 seconds, then gently pull the cream away from the moulds and quickly turn out on to the serving dishes. Add a scoop of pistachio ice cream, scatter with a few pistachios and place the caramelised hazelnuts in each dish at an angle.

walnut and semolina tourte with roasted figs, honeycomb and iced yoghurt

Walnuts and honey are a very common combination in Turkish and Greek desserts, whether made into a cake or simply served with yoghurt. I got the idea for this recipe while eating at a friend's restaurant in Turkey, where we had figs stuffed with walnuts and poached in a honey syrup that was rather too sweet for my taste. I asked for some yoghurt with it so the acidity would cut the sweetness, and when I came home I devised this dish. I have opted for the use of fresh honeycomb here because it adds a different texture, giving the dish another dimension.

Serves 10–12

for the walnut and semolina tourte
220g ground walnuts
50g fine semolina
50g plain flour
1 teaspoon baking powder
3 eggs
200g caster sugar
250g unsalted butter, melted
juice of 2 oranges
grated zest of 1 orange
75g walnuts, roughly broken
icing sugar for dusting

for the iced yoghurt
1 gelatine leaf
250ml double cream
100ml liquid glucose
125g caster sugar
750g homemade yoghurt (follow the recipe
   on page 18, omitting the cardamom)

for the roasted figs
10–12 black mission figs
120g unsalted butter
50g caster sugar
$1/2$ cinnamon stick
25g honey

to serve
10–12 pieces of fresh honeycomb

walnut and semolina tourte
Mix the ground walnuts, semolina, flour and baking powder together and set aside. Whisk the eggs and caster sugar together until thick and pale, then add the melted butter in a thin stream as if making mayonnaise, whisking constantly. Fold in the semolina mixture, followed by the orange juice and zest and the broken walnuts. Transfer the mixture to a buttered lined round 23cm springform cake tin and place in an oven preheated to 160°C/ Gas Mark 3. Bake for 40 minutes; the cake should still be slightly underdone in the middle so the cooling process will finish it off. Allow to cool in the tin for 10 minutes, then turn out on to a wire rack to cool completely. Dust with icing sugar.

iced yoghurt
Soak the gelatine in cold water for about 5 minutes, until soft and pliable, then squeeze out all the water. Put the double cream, glucose and caster sugar in a saucepan and bring to the boil, stirring to dissolve the sugar. Remove from the heat and add the gelatine, stirring until dissolved. Leave to cool for 5 minutes.

Put the yoghurt in a bowl and whisk in the cream mixture. Pass through a fine sieve, then place in an ice-cream machine and freeze according to the manufacturer's instructions. Transfer to the fridge to soften slightly about 10 minutes before serving.

roasted figs
Cut the very top off the figs, then cut them horizontally in half; try to make them as near to the same size as possible.

Heat the butter in a cast-iron pan. When it is foaming, add the figs, cut-side down, and cook over a medium-high heat for 2–3 minutes to get a little colour. Remove the figs from the pan and set aside. Add the sugar, cinnamon and honey to the pan and cook for 3–4 minutes, until syrupy. Return the figs to the pan, cut-side up, and spoon a little of the syrup over each one. Transfer the pan to an oven preheated to 180°C/ Gas Mark 4 and cook for 5 minutes, spooning the syrup over the figs 2 or 3 times.

serving
Cut the cake into 10–12 slices and place each one on a serving plate with 2 pieces of roasted fig, pouring a little syrup over each one. Add a piece of honeycomb and a scoop of iced yoghurt. If there are any juices left from the figs, you can drizzle these around the plates.

semifreddo of macadamia nuts with passion fruit and star anise sorbet

A semifreddo is a light, partially frozen dessert, particularly suitable for serving on a lazy summer evening. Here, the sharpness of the passion fruit balances the whole thing perfectly.

You could change the type of nut, maybe using almonds, and perhaps add some ground liquorice root or even a little chilli to the sorbet instead of the star anise. The passion fruit syrup could be flavoured with lemongrass or lime leaves – anything to keep the freshness of the dish.

Serves 10

for the nougatine
125g macadamia nuts
50ml water
125g caster sugar

for the semifreddo of macadamia nuts
250g caster sugar
juice and grated zest of 1 lime
75ml water
4 egg yolks
3 egg whites
350ml double cream
125g crystallised ginger, chopped

for the passion fruit syrup
juice of 1 orange (about 100ml)
100g caster sugar
30ml water
10 passion fruit

for the passion fruit and star anise sorbet
200ml fresh orange juice
150g caster sugar
4 star anise
50ml liquid glucose
1^1/$_2$ gelatine leaves
500ml passion fruit juice

nougatine
Scatter the macadamia nuts on to a baking tray, place in an oven preheated to 200°C/ Gas Mark 6 and roast for about 5 minutes, until golden brown. Remove from the oven and leave to cool.

Put the water and sugar in a heavy-based pan and heat gently, stirring to dissolve the sugar. Bring to the boil and cook without stirring until the syrup turns into a rich, golden-brown caramel. Immediately add the nuts and stir until they are well coated in the caramel. Tip the mixture out of the pan on to an oiled baking sheet, spread it out a little and leave to cool. When it is cold and set, place it in a bowl and smash roughly with the end of a rolling pin, being careful not to turn it into a powder. Store in an airtight container until needed.

semifreddo of macadamia nuts
Put 175g of the caster sugar in a heavy-based pan with the lime zest and water and heat gently, stirring to dissolve the sugar. Raise the heat, bring to the boil and cook without stirring until it reaches 121°C on a sugar thermometer – the syrup should just be starting to change colour. Meanwhile, place the egg yolks in a freestanding electric mixer and whisk on high speed until thick and pale. When the sugar syrup reaches the correct temperature, pour it on to the egg yolks in a slow, steady stream, whisking all the time. Keep whisking until the mixture is cool; it should be creamy white and very thick.

In a separate bowl, whisk the egg whites with the lime juice until frothy. Add 25g of the caster sugar and whisk to soft peaks. Add the remaining sugar and beat well.

Whip the cream to a light ribbon stage, allowing a pattern to form and hold its shape but being careful not to overwhip it. Fold the cream into the egg yolk mixture, then fold in the egg whites. Finally, fold in the nougatine and the crystallised ginger. Divide the mixture between 10 dariole moulds, 120ml in capacity, tapping them gently to remove any air pockets that might have formed. Freeze for at least 8 hours.

passion fruit syrup
Place the orange juice, sugar, water and the pulp from 8 of the passion fruit in a saucepan. Bring to the boil, stirring to dissolve the sugar, then simmer for 4–5 minutes. Pass through a fine sieve. While the syrup is still warm, whisk in the pulp from the remaining passion fruit. Leave to cool, then store in the fridge.

passion fruit and star anise sorbet
Place the orange juice, caster sugar, star anise and glucose in a saucepan and bring to the boil, stirring to dissolve the sugar. Lower the heat and simmer for 4 minutes. Meanwhile, soak the gelatine in cold water for about 5 minutes, until soft and pliable.

Remove the pan from the heat. Squeeze all the water out of the gelatine, then add the gelatine to the pan and stir until dissolved. Leave to cool. Stir in the passion fruit juice and pass the mixture through a fine sieve. Freeze in an ice-cream machine according to the manufacturer's instructions. Transfer to the fridge to soften slightly about 10 minutes before serving.

serving
Remove the semifreddo from the freezer, dip the moulds in hot water for 2–3 seconds and then turn out on to serving plates. Coat completely with the passion fruit syrup and serve with a scoop of sorbet on top.

white chocolate, banana and peanut bread pudding with chestnut honey ice cream

This is one of those extremely rich desserts that you feel very naughty about eating after the deed! The nuts give the pudding a little texture. When choosing chestnut honey for the ice cream, please use the best you can find, as it really does make a difference.

The nice thing about this dessert is that it can be eaten warm or cold – my preference is warm.

Serves 10–12

for the chestnut honey ice cream
500ml milk
200ml double cream
120g chestnut honey
5 egg yolks
25g milk powder
30g caster sugar

for the banana tuiles
100g banana flesh (about 2 bananas),
  whizzed in a liquidiser to make a purée
20ml lemon juice
20g rice flour
20g unsalted butter, melted

for the caramelised bananas
2 bananas
25g caster sugar

for the bread pudding
750ml double cream
50g smooth peanut butter
450g white chocolate, chopped
75g unsalted butter
75g Demerara sugar
3 bananas, sliced
2 eggs
4 egg yolks

250g crustless white bread, preferably
  1–2 days old, cut into 1cm dice
100g roasted and skinned peanuts

chestnut honey ice cream
Put the milk, cream and chestnut honey in a heavy-based saucepan and bring gently to just below the boil. Meanwhile, whisk the egg yolks, milk powder and sugar together until pale and creamy. Pour half the milk mixture on to the eggs, whisking until combined, then pour it back into the pan. Cook over a gentle heat, stirring constantly with a wooden spoon, until the mixture thickens enough to coat the back of the spoon (it should register about 84°C on a sugar thermometer). Strain immediately through a fine sieve into a large bowl to help stop the cooking. When cool, freeze in an ice-cream machine according to the manufacturer's instructions. Transfer to the fridge to soften slightly about 10 minutes before serving.

banana tuiles
Place all the ingredients in a bowl and beat well. Cover and place in the fridge for 2–3 hours to set a little.

Spread the mixture out on a sheet of baking parchment in 2 x 6cm strips. Transfer to a lined baking sheet, place in an oven preheated to 180°C/Gas Mark 4 and bake for 5 minutes, until golden. Remove from the oven and leave to cool on the baking sheet. Store in an airtight container.

caramelised bananas
Peel the bananas and slice each one across into 10–12 pieces. Lay them on a baking sheet and dust with the sugar. Melt the sugar on each slice with a blowtorch until deep golden brown, then leave to cool.

bread pudding
Pour the double cream into a saucepan, bring to the boil and then remove from the heat. Add the peanut butter, whisking until dissolved. Leave to cool for a couple of minutes, then pour the mixture on to 350g of the chopped chocolate. Stir until all the chocolate has melted, then cool.

Heat the butter in a frying pan until foaming, then add the Demerara sugar and cook for 2–3 minutes. Add the bananas and cook until golden. Remove from the heat and leave to cool.

Whisk the eggs and egg yolks together, then pour in the chocolate cream mix, whisking until combined. Strain through a fine sieve into a bowl, add the diced bread and mix well. Put to one side for about 20 minutes, so the bread can absorb the custard. Then carefully mix in the remaining chopped chocolate, the bananas and two-thirds of the peanuts. Place the mixture in a buttered, lined 30 x 20 x 3cm baking tray and sprinkle the remaining peanuts over the top. Put the tray in a large roasting tin, then pour enough hot water into the tin to come half way up the sides of the tray. Place in an oven preheated to 180°C/ Gas Mark 4 and cook for 30–40 minutes, until the mixture is golden and feels firm to the touch; a knife inserted in the centre should come out clean. Remove from the roasting tin and cool for 5 minutes before serving.

serving
Cut the warm bread pudding into portions and serve with a scoop of ice cream, a couple of pieces of caramelised banana and a banana tuile.

chocolate brownies

This is a dish that has evolved over time. Originally it was just the brownie base, served slightly underdone so it was still goocy in the centre. To refine it, we added a chocolate cream. It is loosely based on a chocolate brûlée that we make sometimes, and you could, if you like, infuse it with rose geranium or lavender for a subtly different flavour. Finally came the rich glaze, topped with crisp chocolate caramel strands to add texture – and that's how our chocolate brownie was created.

I serve it on its own, but if you would prefer an accompaniment, a Sichuan peppercorn ice cream or even liquorice ice cream would be in keeping with the dark flavours of this dessert.

Serves 10–12

for the chocolate brownies
2 eggs
175g caster sugar
240g bitter chocolate (64 per cent cocoa solids)
150g unsalted butter, melted
seeds from 1 vanilla pod
20g cocoa powder
$1/2$ teaspoon baking powder
60g plain flour
100g hazelnuts, toasted, skinned and finely chopped
100g bitter chocolate (71 per cent cocoa solids), finely chopped

for the chocolate cream
400ml double cream
400ml milk
130g egg yolks (about 4)
100g caster sugar
500g bitter chocolate (71 per cent cocoa solids), chopped

for the chocolate glaze
150ml water
175g caster sugar
55g bitter cocoa powder
125ml double cream
$2^{1}/_{3}$ gelatine leaves
40g bitter chocolate (64 per cent cocoa solids), chopped

for the chocolate strands
100g fondant
100ml liquid glucose
100g isomalt (available from MSK, see page 148, and also sometimes from healthfood shops)
70g bitter chocolate (64 per cent cocoa solids), chopped

chocolate brownies
Whisk the eggs and sugar together until thick and pale. Put the 64 per cent chocolate in a large bowl and melt over a pan of simmering water or in a microwave (see page 23). Stir in the melted butter and vanilla, then fold in the egg mixture. Sift together the cocoa powder, baking powder and flour and fold them in too. Add the nuts and chopped chocolate, then transfer the mixture to a greased and lined 12 x 36 x 4cm baking tray and place in an oven preheated to 180°C/Gas Mark 4. Bake for 20–25 minutes, until just cooked but still a little soft in the middle. Remove from the oven and leave to cool while you make the chocolate cream.

chocolate cream
Bring the cream and milk to the boil in a heavy-based saucepan, then remove from the heat. Whisk the egg yolks and sugar together, then pour on the cream, whisking to combine. Return the mixture to the saucepan and cook gently for 2 minutes.

Put the chopped chocolate in a bowl and pour on the cream mixture, whisking until the chocolate has dissolved. Pass through a fine sieve. Press the edge of the brownie against the sides of the tin to make sure there aren't any gaps, then immediately pour on the warm chocolate cream, leaving a 2mm gap at the top of the tin for the glaze. Place the tin in an oven preheated to 150°C/Gas Mark 2 and cook for 20–25 minutes, keeping your eye on it. The cream should be just set and wobble very slightly in the middle. Remove from the oven, allow to cool for 3–4 minutes and then stretch a piece of cling film over the tin; this will allow the cream to finish cooking in its residual heat. When it is completely cold, place in the fridge for 1 hour.

chocolate glaze
Put the water and caster sugar in a saucepan and bring to the boil, stirring to dissolve the sugar. Whisk in the cocoa powder and cream, bring back to the boil, then turn the heat down and simmer for 10 minutes.

Soak the gelatine in cold water for about 5 minutes, until soft and pliable, then squeeze out all the water. Remove the pan from the heat and add the gelatine, stirring until dissolved. Leave to cool for 3–4 minutes, then pour on to the chopped chocolate, whisking until it has melted. Pass through a fine sieve and leave to cool.

Remove the brownie from the fridge and spread a layer of the cooled glaze on top, smoothing the surface so it is level with the top of the tin. Return to the fridge to set.

chocolate strands

Place the fondant, glucose and isomalt in a heavy-based saucepan, stir well and bring to the boil. Cook until just before the sugar is starting to turn colour (160–165°C on a sugar thermometer). Remove from the heat, add the chocolate and stir until dissolved. Pour out on to an oiled baking tray and cool slightly. While it is still very warm, slowly pull off little pieces; they should form strands about 4–6cm long.

Snip them off with scissors and lay them on a tray until needed; be careful, they will be very brittle. If you are keeping them for any length of time, store in an airtight container. Any leftover pieces can be ground to a powder in a food processor and kept in a small jar. Then when you need some, you can sprinkle the powder evenly over a lined baking tray and place in the oven to melt. You can then make more strands or place a piece of baking parchment on top, roll out the mixture as thinly as possible and then cut it, or let it cool and break it into uneven shapes.

serving

Carefully remove the brownie from the tin and cut it into portions, using a warm, wet knife. Place on serving plates and arrange some chocolate strands on top.

tanzanian chocolate ganache with white chocolate mousse

This is a relatively easy dessert to prepare, with the ingredients left as a blank canvas so the flavours ring true. I have used Tanzanian chocolate, which has a fruity, floral taste and is wonderfully rich. If you can't obtain Tanzanian chocolate try to find the best quality you can, with 75 per cent cocoa solids.

You could add other flavours to the mousses: try bergamot, lavender, wild thyme or lime with the dark chocolate one and black pepper, sorrel, coffee or roses for the white chocolate.

Serves 6

for the white chocolate mousse
400ml double cream
3 egg yolks
25g caster sugar
3 gelatine leaves
500g white chocolate

for the Tanzanian chocolate ganache:
200ml double cream
50g unsalted butter
400g Tanzanian chocolate, chopped

for the dark chocolate shapes
250g bitter chocolate (64 per cent cocoa solids), chopped
120ml walnut oil

white chocolate mousse
Whip 300ml of the double cream until it forms soft ribbons on the surface. Put to one side.

Place the egg yolks and sugar in a bowl and set it over a pan of simmering water, making sure the water doesn't touch the base of the bowl. Whisk until thick and creamy, then set aside.

Soak the gelatine in cold water for about 5 minutes, until soft and pliable. Remove and squeeze out all the water. Bring the remaining cream to the boil in a small saucepan, then remove from the heat and add the gelatine, stirring until dissolved.

Melt the white chocolate in a bowl set over a pan of simmering water or in a microwave (see page 23). Stir in the cream and gelatine mixture, then fold in the egg yolk mixture. Allow to cool a little, then fold in the double cream a third at a time. Cover and leave in the fridge for at least 4 hours, preferably overnight.

tanzanian chocolate ganache
Put the double cream in a saucepan, bring to the boil, then remove from the heat. Whisk in the butter until dissolved, then pour this mixture on to the chocolate in a bowl and stir until melted. Leave to cool. When cold, place in the fridge for about 10 minutes, then remove and beat well; it should be stiff enough to pipe but not so cold that it has set.

dark chocolate shapes
Place the chopped chocolate in a bowl and melt over a pan of simmering water or in a microwave (see page 23). When nearly melted, remove from the heat and allow to melt completely. Stir in the walnut oil a third at a time. Pour the chocolate on to a piece of shiny acetate about 30cm square, spread it over evenly, then leave to cool. If you don't have any acetate, a piece of black dustbin liner will do, as long as it is stretched tight.

When the chocolate has set, cut it into 18 equilateral triangles plus 6 thin strips for the top of the white chocolate mousse. Store in an airtight container in a cool place until needed.

serving
Place the chocolate ganache in a piping bag and pipe in lines on 12 of the chocolate triangles. Make 6 piles by stacking them on top of each other, then place the remaining 6 pieces on top. Carefully lift on to serving plates, top with a scoop of white chocolate mousse and then a strip of chocolate. You could melt a little of the ganache to brush on to the plates, as in the picture.

warm chocolate mousse with espresso-soaked sponge and amaretto sabayon

While the photography was being done for this book, a friend called Vlad, who runs Hot Pepper Jelly, a café just down the road from the restaurant, supplied us with vast amounts of fantastic hot chocolate spiced with chilli. It was during this time it occurred to me that it might be fun to do a warm chocolate mousse, so thank you, Vlad. I've kept the flavours straight here but you could add chilli, star anise or orange zest to the chocolate mousse or use Cointreau or Marsala in the sabayon.

When you eat this, make sure you go to the very bottom of the glass to get a little of everything.

Serves 8

for the warm chocolate mousse
400ml double cream
400ml milk
100ml water
25g caster sugar
4.5g carrageen powder
1g locust bean gum (available from MSK, see page 148)
250g bitter chocolate (75 per cent cocoa solids), chopped

for the espresso-soaked sponge
4 Sponge Fingers (see page 131)
400ml hot, strong espresso coffee

for the Amaretto sabayon
4 egg yolks
40g caster sugar
50ml Amaretto di Saronno liqueur

to serve
50g very bitter chocolate (100 per cent cocoa solids)

warm chocolate mousse
Put the double cream, milk and water in a heavy-based saucepan, bring to the boil and then remove from the heat, Mix the caster sugar, carrageen powder and locust bean gum together and whisk into the cream mix. Return to the heat and simmer for 3 minutes. Remove from the heat again, allow to cool for 3 minutes, then pour on to the chopped chocolate and stir until dissolved. Pass through a fine sieve and pour into an Isi cream whipper (see Note on page 88). Charge it with 2 gas cylinders and keep warm at approximately 70°C in a bain marie until needed.

espresso-soaked sponge
Break up the sponge fingers and divide between 8 Irish coffee glasses. Pour on the hot espresso so that it soaks through the sponge.

amaretto sabayon
Put all the ingredients in a round-bottomed bowl and whisk until frothy. Place the bowl over a pan of simmering water, making sure the water doesn't touch the base of the bowl. Whisk with a handheld electric beater until the sabayon is very thick and creamy and has doubled in volume. Use immediately.

serving
Shake the cream whipper and squirt the mousse into the glasses, filling them two-thirds full. Top with the sabayon and grate over the 100 per cent chocolate.

raisin and chocolate financiers with rum and raisin ice cream

These are lovely little warm chocolate cakes – not with a runny middle (they have been done to death), but nice and light with an intense chocolate taste. The raisins add a deep Muscat fruitiness, but could just as easily be replaced by chopped prunes or cranberries. We have even used dried white mulberries that I once brought back from a market in Turkey.

The rum and raisin ice cream matches the raisins in the financiers, but an almond, orange or brown butter ice cream could be used to good effect as well.

Serves 10

for the rum and raisin ice cream
300g raisins
150ml water
100ml good-quality dark rum
600ml double cream
500ml milk
10 egg yolks
150g caster sugar
50ml liquid glucose

for the raisin and chocolate financiers
50g golden raisins, roughly chopped
25ml dark rum
250g unsalted butter, diced
50g plain flour
75g cocoa powder
125g ground almonds
a pinch of salt
285g egg whites (7–8 whites)
250g icing sugar
30g chestnut honey
50g bitter chocolate (71 per cent cocoa solids), roughly chopped
bitter cocoa powder and icing sugar for dusting

rum and raisin ice cream

Place the raisins, water and half the rum in a saucepan and bring to the boil. Remove from the heat, cover and leave until the raisins plump up.

Meanwhile, bring the cream and milk to the boil in a heavy-based pan, then remove from the heat. Whisk the egg yolks, caster sugar and glucose together in a bowl. Pour on half the milk mixture, whisking constantly, then pour the mixture back into the pan. Cook over a low heat, stirring all the time with a wooden spoon, until the mixture thickens enough to coat the back of the spoon (it should register about 84°C on a sugar thermometer). Strain immediately through a fine sieve into a bowl and leave to cool. Add the remaining rum and then strain in the juices from the raisins. Freeze in an ice-cream machine according to the manufacturer's instructions, adding the raisins just before it is ready. Transfer to the fridge to soften slightly about 10 minutes before serving.

raisin and chocolate financiers

Put the raisins and rum in a small saucepan and heat gently. Remove from the heat, cover and leave until the raisins plump up.

Place the butter in a frying pan over a medium heat and cook until golden brown. Cool quickly and then pour through a fine sieve into a bowl. Set aside.

Sift the flour and cocoa powder into a bowl, add the ground almonds and salt and mix well.

Briefly mix the egg whites with the sugar, then add the cocoa mixture, stirring well. Mix in the butter and honey, followed by the chopped chocolate, raisins and any juices that are left. Cover and leave in the fridge overnight.

Grease 10 rectangular moulds, 10 x 5 x 3cm. Divide the mixture between the moulds, filling them two-thirds full, then place in an oven preheated to 180°C/Gas Mark 4 and bake for 10 minutes, until a skewer inserted in the centre comes out clean. Remove from the oven and cool for a couple of minutes, then turn the cakes out of the moulds. Dust with cocoa powder and then dust lightly with icing sugar.

serving

Serve the financiers accompanied by a scoop of ice cream.

bitter chocolate and black olive tarts with fennel ice cream

Olives seem to bring out the flavour of chocolate and vice versa, with the chocolate emphasising the fruit of the olive. This dessert is becoming a favourite with our customers. If you don't like the idea of the olives they could be left out, but do try it, please.

Serves 8

for the sugared black olives
200g caster sugar
250ml water
juice of 1 lemon
500g black olives in brine, well drained and stoned

for the fennel ice cream
500ml milk
500ml double cream
275g fennel, chopped
8 egg yolks
185g caster sugar
50ml liquid glucose
25ml Pernod

for the olive tuiles
125g sugared black olives (see below), drained and chopped
250ml liquid glucose
175g isomalt (available from MSK, see page 148, and from some healthfood shops)
25ml water

for the bitter chocolate and black olive tarts
200g bitter chocolate (71 per cent cocoa solids), chopped
100g unsalted butter, diced
100ml olive oil
75g plain flour
50g extra bitter cocoa powder
6 eggs
150g caster sugar
200g sugared black olives (see below), chopped
cocoa powder for dusting

sugared black olives
Place the caster sugar, water and lemon juice in a large saucepan and bring to the boil, stirring to dissolve the sugar. Add the olives and simmer over a low heat for 5 minutes. Remove from the heat and leave to cool. Store in a sealed container overnight, covered with the syrup, before use.

fennel ice cream
Put the milk, cream and fennel in a heavy-based saucepan and bring gently to just below the boil. Remove from the heat and leave to infuse for 2 hours or even overnight.

Gently bring to the boil again. Meanwhile, whisk the egg yolks with the sugar and glucose until pale and creamy. Pour half the milk mixture on to the eggs, whisking to combine, then pour back into the saucepan. Cook over a gentle heat, stirring constantly with a wooden spoon, until the mixture thickens enough to coat the back of the spoon (it should register 84°C on a thermometer). Remove from the heat, push through a fine sieve and leave to cool. Stir in the Pernod, then place in an ice-cream machine and freeze according to the manufacturer's instructions. Transfer to the fridge to soften slightly about 10 minutes before serving.

olive tuiles
Scatter the sugared olives over a baking sheet lined with baking parchment. Leave in an oven preheated to 90°C (or the lowest possible gas mark) for 3–4 hours, until the olives look dried out and wizened. Cool and store in an airtight container.

Place the glucose, isomalt and water in a heavy-based saucepan and dissolve over a gentle heat. Bring to the boil and cook without stirring until caramelised; it should be a golden amber colour. Immediately add the chopped black olives and pour the mixture on to an oiled baking tray. Put to one side until cold and very crisp. Break the caramel up, place in a food processor and pulse to a coarse powder. Store in an airtight container.

When needed, sprinkle the craquant over a lined baking tray in an even layer to create a 16 x 20cm rectangle. Place in an oven preheated to 200°C/Gas Mark 6 until it has melted and formed a single sheet of caramel. Remove from the oven, leave to cool and, just before it sets, cut it into equilateral triangles with 4cm sides. If it sets too quickly, return it to the oven until just soft again.

Any left over can be kept in an airtight container for future use. It is lovely folded through an ice cream.

bitter chocolate tarts
Place the chopped chocolate in a bowl and melt over a pan of simmering water or in a microwave (see page 23) until fluid.

Whisk the butter into the warm chocolate bit by bit, waiting until each piece has been amalgamated before adding the next. Then gradually whisk in the olive oil. This stage is very important. Do not be tempted to put the chocolate, butter and oil in the bowl all at once and heat together, or the tart won't rise as well.

Sift in the flour and cocoa powder and beat well. Then whisk the eggs with the sugar, just to break them down a little, and mix them into the chocolate. Finally mix in the chopped olives.

Divide the mixture between 8 lined loose-bottomed tart tins, 9cm in diameter and 3cm deep, filling them to within 2–3mm of the top. Place on a baking sheet and bake in an oven preheated to 180°C/Gas Mark 4 for 6–7 minutes. The tarts should be slightly underdone in the centre. Remove from the oven and leave to rest for 2 minutes before unmoulding.

serving
Unmould the tarts, dust with cocoa powder and carefully plate. Add a scoop of fennel ice cream and top with an olive tuile.

chocolate délice with salted caramel and malted barley ice cream

This has now become a bit of a classic at the restaurant. It featured in my first book, *Essence* (Absolute Press, 2006), but always receives such rave reviews from customers that I decided to include it in this one as well. It is just one of those desserts that is spot on.

The caramel could be replaced with a flavoured pastry cream filling – a rose geranium one works very well. Just remember to loosen your pastry cream a little to give the consistency of a thick custard.

Serves 8

for the malted barley ice cream
125g pearl barley
250ml double cream
500ml milk
1 vanilla pod, slit open lengthwise
5 egg yolks
50g caster sugar
75g malt extract

for the sesame wafers
25g golden syrup
75g Demerara sugar
25ml milk
75g unsalted butter
25g ground almonds
30g sesame seeds

for the salted caramel
250g granulated sugar
25ml water
150ml double cream
150g unsalted butter, diced
Maldon salt, to taste

for the chocolate délice
300g bitter chocolate (64–71 per cent cocoa solids), chopped, plus 125g bitter chocolate for the chocolate discs
25g unsalted butter
1/2 gelatine leaf
25ml hot water
2 egg yolks
5g bitter cocoa powder
200ml olive oil
145g egg whites (about 5)

malted barley ice cream
Spread the pearl barley out on a baking tray and place in an oven preheated to 180°C/Gas Mark 4. Toast for about 5 minutes, until golden brown.

Put the cream, milk and split vanilla pod into a heavy-based pan, add the toasted barley and bring to the boil. Remove from the heat and leave to infuse for 30–40 minutes. Place back on the heat and bring back to the boil. Whisk the egg yolks, caster sugar and malt extract together in a bowl, then pour in half the hot milk mixture, whisking continuously. Return the mixture to the pan and cook on a low heat, stirring constantly with a wooden spoon, until the mixture thickens enough to coat the back of the spoon (it should register about 84°C on a thermometer). Do not let it boil or it will become scrambled. Immediately strain through a fine sieve into a bowl and leave to cool. Pour into an ice-cream machine and freeze according to the manufacturer's instructions. Transfer to the fridge to soften slightly about 10 minutes before serving.

sesame wafers
Put the golden syrup and Demerara sugar in a small pan and heat gently until the sugar has dissolved. Add the milk and leave to cool a little. Mix in the butter, ground almonds and sesame seeds. Place in the fridge for 30 minutes.

Spread the mixture on to a baking sheet lined with baking parchment, keeping it away from the edges as it will expand during cooking. Bake in an oven preheated to 180°C/Gas Mark 4 for 4–5 minutes, until golden brown. Remove from the oven and leave to cool. Carefully break into the desired shape; we create random jagged pieces. Store in a sealed container until needed; the wafers can be made 3–4 days in advance.

salted caramel
Put the sugar and water in a heavy-based pan and heat gently, stirring, until the sugar has dissolved. Raise the heat and cook without stirring until a rich, deep golden caramel is obtained, being careful not to take it too far or it will be bitter. The moment you are happy with the colour, remove the pan from the heat and pour in the double cream little by little; take care, as it will spit. Whisk until the caramel has dissolved. Cool slightly, then whisk in the butter a little at a time. Add the salt to your taste; start off with a pinch and gradually increase it until you achieve a slight saltiness. Leave to cool completely.

chocolate délice

Place the 300g chopped chocolate in a bowl and melt over a pan of simmering water or in a microwave (see page 23). Stir in the butter, then place the bowl to one side, keeping it warm.

Soak the gelatine in cold water for about 5 minutes, until soft and pliable. Put the hot water in a small bowl. Squeeze out all the water from the gelatine and add it to the hot water, stirring until dissolved. Set aside.

Whisk the egg yolks together and mix in the cocoa powder. Slowly drizzle in the olive oil a little at a time, whisking constantly, as if making mayonnaise. Stir in the gelatine water and then carefully add the mixture to the chocolate. Whisk the egg whites briefly, just to break them down (they should not be white and frothy), then carefully fold them into the chocolate mixture. Pour the mixture into 8 metal rings, 5cm in diameter and 5cm high, filling them two thirds full. Chill for 2 hours, until set. Keep the remaining chocolate mixture at room temperature.

When the chocolate has set, push it up the sides of the moulds with your fingers so a well is formed in the centre. Pour in the salted caramel to just below the top of the mould. Place a chocolate disc on top and cover with the remaining chocolate mix. Return to the fridge until needed. They will keep for 3–4 days.

chocolate discs

Melt the extra 125g chocolate as described above. Spread it out on a sheet of cellophane (you can even use a black bin bag) and leave to set. Cut into eight 4cm discs with a metal cutter.

serving

Unmould the chocolate délice either by flashing a blowtorch quickly over the rings or by rolling them in the heat of your hands to release the mousse. Invert on to 8 serving plates. Place a scoop of ice cream on each plate and stud with a sesame wafer.

fruit

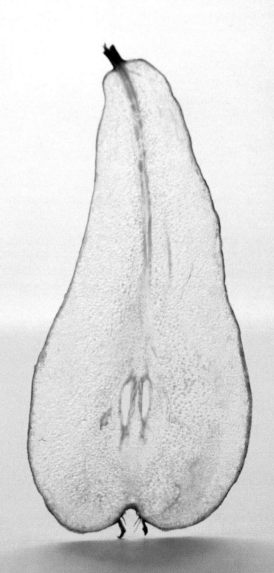

There is a bountiful supply of fruit grown in the UK: greengages, damsons, rhubarb, the best strawberries in the world, plus apples, pears and plums galore. I have chosen to concentrate on my particular favourites in this chapter. Always remember that fruit is at its best when in season: there are juicy peaches, apricots and red, aromatic strawberries in summer, plums, pears and apples for warm, comforting desserts in autumn and winter. I see little point in using raspberries, for example, that have been grown out of season and haven't been warmed by the sun, which helps develop their natural sugars and make them more flavoursome.

'...there are juicy peaches, apricots and red, aromatic strawberries in summer, plums, pears and apples for warm, comforting desserts in autumn and winter.'

strawberry and hibiscus jelly with lemon verbena custard and blackcurrant sorbet

We like to serve this as a pre-dessert in summer. We use the ripest English strawberries and set them in a jelly made with dried hibiscus flowers, which are deep ruby red and have a tart taste with a hint of rhubarb and raspberry. The lemon verbena custard and blackcurrant sorbet have a light, palate-cleansing effect.

This dessert is illustrated on the book jacket.

Serves 10 as a pre-dessert

for the strawberry and hibiscus jelly
juice of 1 orange
juice of 1/2 lemon
25g dried hibiscus (available from some healthfood shops)
75g caster sugar
3 gelatine leaves
250g strawberries, cut into small dice

for the lemon verbena custard
50g lemon verbena leaves, roughly chopped
120ml lemon juice
550ml double cream
100ml milk
2 1/4 gelatine leaves
100g caster sugar

for the blackcurrant sorbet
750g blackcurrants
200g caster sugar
200ml water
25ml liquid glucose
1 gelatine leaf
juice of 1/2 lemon

strawberry and hibiscus jelly
Put the orange and lemon juice in a measuring jug and add enough water to make it up to 500ml. Pour it into a saucepan, add the hibiscus and caster sugar and bring to the boil, stirring to dissolve the sugar. Simmer for 1 minute, then remove from the heat and leave to infuse for 10 minutes. Meanwhile, soak the gelatine in cold water for about 5 minutes, until soft and pliable.

Bring the hibiscus mixture back to the boil, then remove from the heat. Squeeze all the water out of the gelatine. Whisk the gelatine into the hibiscus mixture until dissolved, then pass it through a fine sieve, pushing as much of the juice through as you can. Leave to cool.

Place the diced strawberries in serving glasses, filling them a third full, then add enough hibiscus jelly just to cover. Place in the fridge for about 6 hours, until set.

lemon verbena custard
Place the verbena and lemon juice in a medium saucepan and bring to the boil. Add the cream and milk and bring to the boil again, then remove from the heat and leave to infuse for 1 hour.

Soak the gelatine leaves in cold water for about 5 minutes, until soft and pliable, then squeeze out all the water. Place the pan back on a gentle heat and add the sugar and gelatine. Whisk until they have dissolved, then strain the mixture through a fine sieve into a bowl, pushing as much of the juice from the leaves through as you can. Leave to cool.

When the hibiscus jelly has set, top it with the lemon verbena custard so that the glasses are two-thirds full, then return to the fridge to set. At this stage they can be left overnight.

blackcurrant sorbet
Place the blackcurrants, sugar, water and glucose in a large saucepan and bring to the boil, stirring to dissolve the sugar. Cook for 5 minutes, until the blackcurrants have broken down, then remove from the heat and liquidise to a smooth purée. Pass through a fine sieve.

Soak the gelatine in cold water for about 5 minutes, until soft and pliable, then squeeze out all the water. Mix the softened gelatine into the blackcurrant purée and heat gently, stirring until dissolved. Add the lemon juice and leave to cool. Pour into an ice-cream machine and freeze according to the manufacturer's instructions. Transfer to the fridge to soften slightly about 10 minutes before serving.

serving
Place the blackcurrant sorbet in a piping bag with a large star tube. Top each glass of jelly and custard with a spiral of blackcurrant sorbet and serve straight away.

damson and orange clafoutis with damson kernel ice cream

This French dessert is traditionally made with cherries but I like to use local damsons. The kernels can be extracted from the stones to make an ice cream; their bitter almond flavour complements the sweet clafoutis perfectly. If you can't get damsons, you could use apricots, greengages or plums instead. Or you could use figs and serve the clafoutis with a fig ice cream. If you don't want to make ice cream, clotted cream is also a good accompaniment.

Serves 6

for the damson and orange clafoutis
36–42 damsons, depending on size
75g ground almonds
25g plain flour, plus extra for dusting
grated zest of 1 orange
a pinch of salt
150g caster sugar
3 eggs
4 egg yolks
350ml double cream
50ml milk
icing sugar for dusting

for the damson kernel ice cream
400ml double cream
500ml milk
15 damson kernels from the damsons for the clafoutis, crushed (use nutcrackers to extract the kernels from the stones)
10 egg yolks
20g milk powder
140g caster sugar
25ml liquid glucose

damson and orange clafoutis
Wash and stone the damsons, keeping 15 of the stones for the ice cream.

Spread the ground almonds out on a baking tray, place in an oven preheated to 180°C/Gas Mark 4 and bake for 3 minutes to dry them out a little. Remove from the oven and leave to cool.

Place the almonds in a mixing bowl with the flour, orange zest, salt and caster sugar. Add the eggs and yolks and whisk till combined, then add the cream and milk and whisk well to make a smooth batter. Leave to rest for at least 6 hours, preferably overnight.

Butter six 11–12cm straight-sided tart tins and line the base and sides with baking parchment. Place them on a baking sheet. Lightly dust the damsons with a little flour and then shake off all the excess; it really has to be just the finest of coatings. Divide the damsons between the tart tins, pour over the batter and then place the baking sheet and tart tins in the oven at 180°C/Gas Mark 4. Bake for about 15 minutes, until the clafoutis have risen and set. Remove from the oven, leave to cool in the tins for 2–3 minutes, then turn out.

damson kernel ice cream
Place the cream, milk and damson kernels in a heavy-based saucepan. Gently bring to just below boiling point, then remove from the heat and leave to infuse for 2 hours or even overnight. Gently bring to just below boiling point again. Meanwhile, whisk the egg yolks, milk powder, sugar and glucose together in a bowl until pale and creamy.

Gradually pour half the milk mixture on to the egg yolks, whisking to incorporate, then pour this back into the saucepan.

Cook over a gentle heat, stirring constantly with a wooden spoon, until the mixture thickens enough to coat the back of the spoon (it should register about 84°C on a thermometer). Remove from the heat and immediately strain through a fine sieve into a large bowl; this helps stop the cooking process. Leave to cool, then pour into an ice-cream machine and freeze according to the manufacturer's instructions. Transfer to the fridge to soften slightly about 10 minutes before serving.

serving
Dust the clafoutis with icing sugar and serve warm, with a scoop of damson kernel ice cream on top.

rhubarb and duck egg custard tart

My Aunt Pat used to make the most wonderful custard – very rich and thick, with the most intense yellow colour you could imagine. She used eggs from a farm just down the road that had yolks of the deepest orange, and served it with stewed rhubarb from the garden.

So this tart is in homage to my aunt. I have used duck eggs to achieve the richness and colour that I remember, and added a layer of thick rhubarb purée to the base. It takes me back to the days I used to spend with her.

Serves 12–14

for the rhubarb purée
1kg rhubarb, cut into 1cm lengths
100g unsalted butter
17.5g caster sugar
2 slices of fresh ginger

for the duck egg custard tart
1 quantity of Sweet Pastry (see page 19)
800ml double cream
11 duck egg yolks
110g caster sugar
1 teaspoon ground ginger
1 heaped teaspoon ground nutmeg

to serve
clotted cream

rhubarb purée
Place all the ingredients for the purée in a saucepan and cook over a very low heat for about 30 minutes, stirring occasionally. It should be quite dry. Remove and discard the ginger, then place the rhubarb in a liquidiser and blend to a smooth purée. Pass through a fine sieve, pushing through as much as you can with a wooden spoon. Set aside to cool.

duck egg custard tart
Roll out the pastry on a lightly floured work surface and use to line a buttered loose-bottomed tart tin, 22cm in diameter and 3–3.5cm deep. Chill for 40–50 minutes, then prick the base with a fork.

Line the pastry case with baking parchment and fill with rice or baking beans. Place on a baking sheet in an oven preheated to 180°C/Gas Mark 4 and bake blind for 10–15 minutes, until very lightly coloured. Carefully remove the paper and beans.

Spread two-thirds of the rhubarb purée over the base of the pastry case and return it to the oven for 5 minutes to get a little skin on top of the rhubarb. Meanwhile, make the duck egg custard. Pour the cream into a saucepan and bring to the boil.

Lightly whisk the egg yolks and sugar together in a bowl. Gradually pour the cream on to this mixture, whisking constantly, then pour it back into the saucepan. Heat through gently, stirring all the time, for about 2 minutes (you do not need to cook the custard at this stage, just raise the temperature so the tart will cook quicker and more evenly). Strain the custard through a fine sieve and carefully pour it into the pastry case. Sprinkle with the ground ginger and nutmeg.

Place the tart in the oven and cook for 20–30 minutes, until the filling is just set.

Remove from the oven and cover with a baking tray for 10 minutes in order to complete the cooking. Remove the baking tray and leave the tart to cool completely.

serving
Cut the tart into slices and serve with the remaining rhubarb purée and a scoop of clotted cream.

white peaches in a red wine and raspberry jus with red wine and raspberry granita

This is a perfect summer dessert, both refreshing and light. The secret of this dish lies in using fruits at their perfect stage of ripeness, while juicy, plump and flavoursome

If you prefer, you could change the flavourings in the granita. Mint is good, and long pepper (a slightly sweet, very hot pepper from Indonesia) could be added. You could also replace the raspberries with blackberries, although I do prefer raspberries.

Serves 8

red wine and raspberry granita
1 bottle of good red wine
150g raspberries
275g caster sugar
juice of 1 lemon
100ml water

for the white peaches
350ml red wine
350ml sparkling water
125g caster sugar
2 strips of orange zest
2cm piece of cinnamon stick
2cm piece of dried liquorice root
20 lemon verbena leaves
300g raspberries
juice of 1/2 lemon
8 white peaches, skinned

red wine and raspberry granita
Place all the ingredients in a large saucepan and bring to the boil, stirring to dissolve the sugar. Cook for 1 minute, then remove from the heat. Pass through a fine sieve, pushing through as much of the raspberry pulp as possible, and leave to cool. Pour into a shallow container and place in the freezer for 2–3 hours, until the mixture has started to freeze around the sides. Using a fork, push the outside into the middle, then even the surface and replace in the freezer. Repeat after 2 hours and continue until the mixture consists of even ice crystals.

white peaches
Put the wine, water, sugar, orange zest, cinnamon, liquorice and half the lemon verbena in a large saucepan and bring to the boil, stirring to dissolve the sugar. Simmer for 15–20 minutes, then remove from the heat and leave to infuse for 2 hours. Pass through a fine sieve and chill. Place in a liquidiser with 100g of the raspberries and the lemon juice. Liquidise until smooth, then pass through a fine sieve again.

Cut the peaches in half, remove the stones and slice each peach half into 5. Divide between 8 glass bowls and scatter with the remaining raspberries. Drizzle over the red wine and raspberry jus, then finely shred the remaining lemon verbena and sprinkle it over the top. Place in the fridge to chill.

serving
Remove the peaches from the fridge 5 minutes before serving. Fork over the granita again and place a mound of it in the middle of each serving bowl.

upside-down plum cake with plum sorbet

The variety of plum we use for this is Early River, one of the smaller plums, with a deep-purple skin and lovely golden flesh. It is well worth seeking out for its remarkable scent and flavour when ripe.

Greengages, apricots and damsons would all make excellent substitutes for plums here. If you don't fancy serving the cake with a sorbet, try vanilla or star anise ice cream instead.

Serves 8

for the plum sorbet
1 gelatine leaf
250ml water
120g caster sugar
30ml liquid glucose
about 750g plums, stoned (you will need
   500g stoned plum flesh)
juice of ¹/₂ lemon

for the plum cake
170g unsalted butter
170g caster sugar
24 ripe plums, stoned and cut into quarters
grated zest of 1 orange
seeds from 1 vanilla pod
140g plain flour
a pinch of salt
1 teaspoon baking powder
juice of 1 orange, brought to the boil and
   then cooled
80g ground almonds
2 eggs
200ml milk

plum sorbet
Soak the gelatine leaf in cold water for about 5 minutes, until soft and pliable. Remove and squeeze out all the water. Put the water, caster sugar and glucose in a saucepan and bring to the boil, stirring to dissolve the sugar. Boil for 3 minutes, then remove from the heat, add the gelatine and stir until dissolved. Leave to cool.

Place the stoned plums in a liquidiser and blend to a purée. Add the sugar syrup and lemon juice and continue to blend to a smooth pulp. Push the mixture through a fine sieve, then freeze in an ice-cream machine according to the manufacturer's instructions. Transfer to the fridge to soften slightly about 10 minutes before serving.

plum cake
Melt 70g of the butter and 30g of the caster sugar in a large frying pan and cook over a medium heat until golden. Add the plums and cook for about 3 minutes, until lightly caramelised. Drain and leave to cool.

Grease 8 individual tart tins, 10cm in diameter and 3cm high, and line with baking parchment. Arrange the caramelised plums in the bottom and set aside. Cream together the remaining butter and sugar, then add the orange zest and the seeds from the vanilla pod. Sift in the flour, salt and baking powder and beat well. Stir in the orange juice and ground almonds. Finally add the eggs, followed by the milk, beating until creamy. Divide the mixture between the tart tins, place on a baking sheet and bake in an oven preheated to 180°C/Gas Mark 4 for 15–20 minutes, until golden. Remove from the oven and leave in a warm place for 5 minutes before turning the cakes out; this allows any juices to soak into the cake.

serving
Turn the cakes out on to serving plates while still warm and add a scoop of plum sorbet.

cantaloupe melon soup with watermelon, roasted strawberries and strawberry sorbet

On a hot summer's evening, this dessert is wonderfully light and refreshing. Roasting the strawberries adds a unique dimension to it, giving a contrast of warm and cold, but you could leave them raw. I have used mint in the soup because I like its fresh, cooling effect, but it could be replaced with lemon balm or lemon verbena.

The soup has a Muscat base but champagne or even a chilled Saumur would also work well. This dish is all about lightness and cleansing flavours, so do bear that in mind when experimenting.

Serves 8

for the strawberry sorbet
750g ripe strawberries, hulled and roughly chopped
100g caster sugar
juice of $^1/_2$ lemon
1 gelatine leaf
30ml liquid glucose
30ml water

for the melon soup
1 large, ripe Cantaloupe melon
125g Muscat de Rivesaltes dessert wine
100ml water
juice of $^1/_2$ lemon
10 mint leaves, plus 8 sprigs to garnish

for the roasted strawberries
40g unsalted butter
24 small strawberries, hulled
50g caster sugar
a few grinds of black pepper

to serve
$^1/_2$ large, ripe watermelon, peeled and cut into 8 rectangles, 2cm thick, 5cm wide and 10cm long

strawberry sorbet
Mix the strawberries with the caster sugar and lemon juice, cover and leave in the fridge overnight.

Soak the gelatine in cold water for about 5 minutes, until soft and pliable. Meanwhile, gently heat the glucose and water in a small pan until the glucose has broken down a little. Squeeze all the water out of the gelatine and add the gelatine to the saucepan, stirring until dissolved. Remove from the heat and leave to cool.

Place the glucose syrup in a liquidiser with the strawberries and their juices and blend until smooth. Pass through a fine sieve. Taste and add a little more lemon juice if the mixture is too sweet. Pour into an ice-cream machine and freeze according to the manufacturer's instructions. Transfer to the fridge to soften slightly about 10 minutes before serving.

melon soup
Cut the melon into 6 wedges, remove the skin and seeds and roughly dice the flesh. Place in a liquidiser with the wine, water and lemon juice and blend until smooth.

Pass through a fine sieve into a bowl, add the mint leaves, then cover and place in the fridge. Leave to infuse for 3–4 hours.

roasted strawberries
Melt the butter in an ovenproof frying pan, add the strawberries and sprinkle with the sugar and ground black pepper. Transfer to an oven preheated to 180°C/Gas Mark 4 and cook for 3–4 minutes, until the strawberries are soft but not mushy. Remove from the oven and keep warm.

serving
Put a piece of watermelon in each serving bowl. Remove the melon soup from the fridge, give it a good whisk to bring it back together again and discard the mint leaves. Pour it over the watermelon, then add 2 small scoops of sorbet and 3 roasted strawberries to each bowl. Finish with a sprig of mint.

baked passion fruit cream with caramelised mango and coconut sorbet

This is a lovely combination, the passion fruit cream with its sharp, tangy flavour, the coconut sorbet providing the roundness that the dish requires, while the mango in two different forms just seems to tie both ingredients together. It's perfect for the end of the meal, as it is not too heavy.

If you don't like cardamom, then try star anise instead. The flavour goes well with any sharp-tasting fruit.

Serves 6

for the coconut sorbet
250ml coconut milk
25g coconut powder
150g caster sugar
75ml double cream
40ml liquid glucose
200ml water
$1/_2$ gelatine leaf
25ml Malibu

for the baked passion fruit cream
300ml passion fruit purée
5 cardamom pods, crushed
250ml double cream
2 eggs
3 egg yolks
75g caster sugar, plus 20g sugar for glazing

for the caramelised mango
1 ripe mango
50g caster sugar

for the mango purée and diced mango:
$1/_2$ large, ripe mango
25–30g caster sugar, to taste
juice of 1 lime

coconut sorbet
Place all the ingredients except the gelatine and Malibu in a saucepan. Whisk well and bring to the boil, whisking from time to time. Meanwhile, soak the gelatine in a little cold water for about 5 minutes, until soft and pliable. Remove and squeeze out all the water. When the coconut mixture is boiling, remove from the heat and stir in the gelatine. Pass through a fine sieve and leave to cool, then stir in the Malibu. Pour into an ice-cream machine and freeze according to the manufacturer's instructions. Transfer to the fridge to soften slightly about 10 minutes before serving.

baked passion fruit cream
Grease 6 stainless steel rings 5cm in diameter and 5cm deep. Wrap some cling film tightly around the bases, then wrap in aluminium foil, allowing it to come half way up the sides. Make sure the foil is very close fitting, as the object is to make the bottom airtight.

Put the passion fruit purée in a small saucepan with the crushed cardamom pods and simmer until reduced by half. Add the double cream and bring to the boil, then remove from the heat. Whisk the eggs, egg yolks and sugar together until fully combined. Gradually pour on the passion fruit cream mixture, stirring all the time, then pour back into the saucepan and warm through a little, stirring constantly; you just need to raise the temperature slightly, not cook it. Pour the mixture through a fine sieve.

Line a deep baking tray with a clean J-cloth. Place the moulds in the tray, then pour the passion fruit cream into them. Pour enough hot water into the baking tray to come a third of the way up the sides of the moulds. Carefully place in an oven preheated to 120°C/Gas Mark $1/_2$ and cook for about 30 minutes, until the creams have set. Remove from the oven and leave in the tray to cool. Then remove from the tray, cover and place in the fridge until needed.

caramelised mango
Peel the mango and cut off the flesh in wide slices. Cut 6 good rectangles and dice the rest of the mango. Set the diced mango to one side. Place the rectangles on a tray and sprinkle with the caster sugar. Caramelise with a blowtorch until they are a deep golden colour, then leave to cool.

mango purée and diced mango
Peel the mango and cut the flesh off the stone. Cut half of it into 4mm dice and set aside. Place the remaining mango flesh, including the leftovers from the caramelised mango, in a liquidiser with the sugar and lime juice and blend until smooth. Taste and add more sugar, if necessary. Pass through a fine sieve and keep, covered, in the fridge until needed.

serving
Remove the passion fruit creams from the fridge and take the foil and cling film off the moulds. Sprinkle the creams with the 20g caster sugar and glaze with a blowtorch. Place a slash of mango purée on each serving plate. Run a knife around the edge of each passion fruit cream and lift off the mould. Place on the plates and garnish with a piece of caramelised mango with a scoop of coconut sorbet on top. Finally, scatter with the diced mango.

fig carpaccio with fig ice cream and baked figs

I have loved figs ever since I was a child, when Fig Rolls were one of my favourite teatime biscuits. There is something wonderful about the deep, almost caramelised taste of very ripe figs, and their tiny seeds seem to explode with flavour. They combine well with so many other ingredients – particularly red wine and port, cinnamon, star anise, liquorice root, raspberries and oranges.

The variety I prefer to use is the Black Mission fig. It is without doubt the best, with its purplish-black skin, powerful fragrance and the exquisite taste. Always buy the ripest figs you can find.

Serves 8

for the fig ice cream
400ml milk
300ml double cream
8 of the ripest figs you can find, preferably Black Mission, roughly chopped (discard the stalks)
100ml port
6 egg yolks
100g caster sugar
40ml liquid glucose
juice of $^1/_2$ lemon

for the orange frangipane
65g unsalted butter
65g caster sugar
finely grated zest of $^1/_2$ orange
35g plain flour
65g ground almonds
1 egg, lightly beaten
1 teaspoon Amaretto liqueur

for the fig carpaccio
8 figs, preferably black mission

for the baked figs
8 figs, preferably black mission
25ml port
25g Demerara sugar
50g unsalted butter

to serve
Maury Syrup (see page 17), for drizzling

fig ice cream
Put the milk and cream in a heavy-based saucepan and bring gently to just below the boil. Remove from the heat, add the figs and port and leave to infuse for 2 hours or even overnight.

Gently bring the mixture to the boil again. Meanwhile, whisk the egg yolks with the sugar and glucose until pale and creamy. Pour half the cream mixture on to the egg yolks, whisking to incorporate, then pour this back into the saucepan. Cook over a gentle heat, stirring constantly with a wooden spoon, until the mixture has thickened enough to coat the back of the spoon (it should register about 84°C on a thermometer). Remove from the heat and liquidise until smooth. Strain immediately through a fine sieve into a large bowl, then whisk in the lemon juice and leave to cool. Pour into an ice-cream machine and freeze according to the manufacturer's instructions. Transfer to the fridge to soften slightly about 10 minutes before serving.

orange frangipane
Cream the butter, sugar and orange zest together until pale and fluffy. Sift the flour and almonds into a bowl. Add a little beaten egg to the butter mixture, beating all the time, then add a little of the flour mixture. Repeat until all the flour and egg have been used, then mix in the Amaretto. The mixture should be light, creamy and smooth. Keep in a cool place until needed.

fig carpaccio
Peel each fig, so all you have is a deep red ball of fig with no skin or white flesh. Slice 3–4mm thick and lay the slices on a baking tray lined with cling film so they form a rough rectangle. Place another sheet of cling film on top and carefully bat out the slices, using the flat part of a cleaver or even the bottom of a small saucepan, until the rectangle is 48 x 12cm and 2mm thick.

Place in the freezer for 1 hour to harden up.

baked figs
Cut the very top off the figs. Cut a cross at the top of each fig, slicing about half way down to the bottom. Open the fig out a little, insert a ball of orange frangipane in the centre and reshape the fig again.

Place the port, sugar and butter in a small saucepan, bring to the boil, stirring to dissolve the sugar, and simmer for 3 minutes. Place the figs in an ovenproof dish in which they fit snugly. Pour over the port syrup and transfer to an oven preheated to 200°C/ Gas Mark 6. Bake for 5 minutes, then baste them with the syrup. Bake for another 5 minutes, then remove from the oven and cool slightly, basting once or twice with the juices.

serving
Remove the fig carpaccio from the freezer and take off the top sheet of cling film. Lightly trim any rough edges, then cut in half lengthways and each half into 4 to give eight 12 x 6cm rectangles. Use the cling film to lift the fig up, flip it over on to the centre of the serving plates and discard the cling film.

Place a scoop of fig ice cream on one side of the carpaccio and a warm baked fig on the other. Drizzle with the Maury syrup.

roasted pears with milk purée, croissant ice cream and muscovado and rum jelly

Roasted pears are one of my favourite desserts, particularly when they are sweet and juicy William pears and involve some sort of caramel. I had one of my top-ten desserts of all time at a friend's restaurant, Phil Howard's two-Michelin-starred The Square in London. A mille feuille of roasted pears and caramel ice cream, it was simple but absolutely perfect. The milk purée in this recipe was created to give a rich cream but not quite as rich as clotted cream, and the warm caramel flavour of the jelly helps to tie everything together. The croissants could be replaced by rye bread, Spiced Bread (see page 20) or gingerbread.

Serves 8

for the croissant ice cream
600ml milk
400ml double cream
300g croissants, chopped
6 egg yolks
175g caster sugar
50ml liquid glucose

for the muscovado and rum jelly
260ml water
2g agar agar
50g dark muscovado sugar
40ml rum

for the milk purée
700ml milk
300ml double cream
20g caster sugar
2g carrageen powder

for the roasted pears
200g caster sugar
440ml water
1 vanilla pod, split open lengthwise
juice of 1 lemon
2 strips of orange zest
2 strips of lemon zest
4 large William pears, peeled
60g unsalted butter
50g Demerara sugar

croissant ice cream

Pour the milk and cream into a heavy-based saucepan, bring gently to just below the boil, then remove from the heat. Add the chopped croissants and leave to infuse for 2 hours or even overnight. Liquidise until smooth, then gently bring to the boil again. Meanwhile, whisk the egg yolks with the sugar and glucose until pale and creamy. Pour half the cream mixture on to the egg yolks, whisking to incorporate, then pour this back into the saucepan. Cook over a gentle heat, stirring constantly with a wooden spoon, until the mixture thickens enough to coat the back of the spoon (it should register about 84°C on a sugar thermometer). Strain immediately through a fine sieve into a large bowl to help stop the cooking. Leave to cool, then transfer to an ice-cream machine and freeze according to the manufacturer's instructions. Transfer to the fridge to soften slightly about 10 minutes before serving.

muscovado and rum jelly

Put the water, agar agar and sugar in a small saucepan and leave for 2–3 minutes to allow the agar agar to reconstitute. Place on the stove, bring to the boil and simmer for 2 minutes. Remove from the heat and allow to cool a little, then stir in the rum. Pour the mixture through a fine sieve into a container to a level of 7–8mm. Place in the fridge to set, then cut it into small cubes.

milk purée

Put the milk and double cream into a large, heavy-based saucepan and bring to the boil. Simmer until reduced to 350ml, stirring occasionally to prevent it catching on the bottom of the pan. Remove from the heat.

Mix the caster sugar with the carrageen and then whisk it into the reduced cream mixture. Allow to swell for 2–3 minutes, then bring to the boil again, whisking all the time. Remove from the heat and strain through a fine sieve into a container. Leave to cool, then place in the fridge for about 4 hours, until set. Transfer to a liquidiser and blend until it is the consistency of clotted cream. Cover and store in the fridge until needed.

roasted pears

First you need to poach the pears. Put the sugar, water, split vanilla pod, lemon juice and orange and lemon zest in a saucepan and bring to the boil, stirring to dissolve the sugar. Simmer for 5 minutes, then add the pears; they should be just covered by the liquid. Cover with a circle of baking parchment and simmer for about 15 minutes, until the pears are still firm but just cooked. Remove from the heat and leave the pears in the syrup to cool down. You can now store them in the fridge until needed.

To roast the pears, drain them well, cut them in half and scoop out the core. Heat the butter in a large, cast iron frying pan. When it is frothing, add the pears, cut-side down, and cook for 3–4 minutes, turning once, until a good colour is obtained. Add the Demerara sugar and cook until it has melted. Add 2 tablespoons of water, then transfer the pan to an oven preheated to 180°C/Gas Mark 4 and roast for 10 minutes, basting every 3–4 minutes with the pan juices, until the pears are a deep golden brown. Remove them from the juices and keep warm until needed. Place the pan back on the stove, add 2 more tablespoons of water and bring to the boil, stirring well. Remove from the heat and pass through a fine sieve.

serving

Place a slash of milk purée on each serving plate, then place a warm pear half on top. Put a scoop of ice cream to the side, add the Muscovado jelly and finally drizzle with a little of the juices from the pear pan.

prune and honey cake with pressed apples and mahlab cherry stone ice cream

Prunes have a natural affinity with almonds and apple. Mahlab cherries are a small black variety that grows wild all over the Mediterranean, right across to Turkey, Iran and Syria. It is the dried kernel of the small cherry stone that I use here, capitalising on its bitter almond flavour. They are quite powerful, so do use in moderation. If you have trouble finding them, then try cracking a few normal cherry stones and removing the kernels. About 10 crushed kernels should be enough,

Serves 10–12

for the mahlab cherry stone ice cream
600ml milk
400ml double cream
20g mahlab cherry stones
12 egg yolks
150g caster sugar
20g milk powder
25ml liquid glucose

for the pressed apple terrine
100g unsalted butter
9 Granny Smith apples, peeled, quartered
    and cored
100g caster sugar
200ml apple juice
3 gelatine leaves

for the prune and honey cake
100ml apple juice
200g soft brown sugar
220g honey
300g plain flour
1 teaspoon baking powder
200g ground almonds
300g unsalted butter
4 eggs
50 Marinated Prunes in Armagnac
    (see page 16), stoned, plus 120ml of their
    liquid

for the prune purée
50g Marinated Prunes in Armagnac
    (see page 16), plus 100ml of their liquid

mahlab cherry stone ice cream
Pour the milk and double cream into a heavy-based saucepan and bring gently to the boil. Crush the cherry stones roughly with a pestle and mortar, add them to the milk and leave to infuse for at least 2 hours, preferably overnight.

Place the pan back on the heat and slowly bring to the boil again. Meanwhile, whisk the egg yolks, caster sugar, milk powder and glucose together. Pour half of the milk mixture on to the egg yolks, whisking to combine, then pour it back into the pan. Cook over a low heat, stirring constantly with a wooden spoon, until the mixture is thick enough to coat the back of the spoon (it should register about 84°C on a thermometer). Strain immediately through a fine sieve into a bowl and leave to cool. Pour into an ice-cream machine and freeze according to the manufacturer's instructions. Transfer to the fridge to soften slightly about 10 minutes before serving.

pressed apple terrine
Place half the butter in a large frying pan and heat until frothing. Add half the apples and cook gently, adding half the sugar when they start to colour. When they are a deep golden colour, add half the apple juice and cook for a further 2 minutes. Drain off the juices and reserve. Remove the apples from the pan and set aside. Repeat the entire process with the other half of the ingredients.

Soak the gelatine in cold water for about 5 minutes, then remove and squeeze out all the water. Place the syrup from the apples back on the stove in the frying pan, bring back to the boil, then reduce the heat and add the gelatine. Cook gently for 1 minute, checking to make sure the gelatine has dissolved. Remove from the heat and pass through a fine sieve, then set aside.

Line a 30 x 8 x 5cm terrine dish with a double layer of cling film, letting it overlap the sides. Arrange a layer of apples in the terrine, pour on a third of the apple juices, then repeat twice more until you have used all the apples and juice. Bring the ends of the cling film up over the top of the terrine and seal. Pierce the cling film with a fork in 8 places down the length of the terrine, then place a board and a weight on top to press it a little. Leave in the fridge for at least 6 hours, preferably overnight, until firmly set.

prune and honey cake
Put the apple juice, sugar and honey in a saucepan and warm through over a medium heat, stirring to dissolve the sugar. Remove from the heat and leave to cool.
Sift the flour and baking powder into the bowl of a freestanding electric mixer. Add the ground almonds and butter and mix on slow speed until the mixture resembles breadcrumbs. With the machine running, slowly pour in the apple juice and honey mixture. Add the eggs one at a time, beating well in between each one.

Transfer the mixture to an 18 x 26 x 4cm baking tray lined with baking parchment. Drain the marinated prunes, then arrange them on top in rows. Place in an oven preheated to 180°C/Gas Mark 4 and bake for about 40 minutes, until the cake is a deep golden brown and a skewer inserted in the centre comes out clean. Remove from the oven, prick all over with a skewer and evenly pour on the prune juices. Leave to cool.

prune purée
Place the ingredients in a liquidiser and blend until smooth, then pass through a fine sieve.

serving
Turn the cake out of the tray and cut it into portions. Place a ring of prune purée on each serving plate, then a piece of cake. Carefully turn the apple terrine out of the mould and cut it into slices through the cling film. Remove the cling film and place a slice in the middle of each serving plate. Add a scoop of ice cream.

tapioca with coconut milk and palm sugar, lychee granita and marinated pineapple

Tapioca is a starch extracted from the root of the cassava tree. It has a rather agreeable texture but a neutral taste, so you need to add some flavoursome ingredients when cooking with it. Here it is cooked with a coconut and lime leaf stock and served with a palm sugar syrup. The marinated pineapple is flavoured with lemon balm but you could also try chilli, black pepper or grated ginger. Serving this dish with a granita made of lychees, with their hint of roses, takes the flavours to the next level. It's a wonderfully clean and refreshing dessert, perfect for a hot summer's day.

Serves 6

for the tapioca
125g tapioca
5 lime leaves
1 lemongrass stalk
450ml coconut milk
juice and grated zest of ¹/₂ lime

for the lychee granita
1 gelatine leaf
250ml water
50g caster sugar
400g lychees, peeled and stoned
juice of 1 lime

for the marinated pineapple
¹/₂ ripe pineapple, peeled and cored
30g caster sugar
juice of 1 lime
8 lemon balm leaves, shredded

for the palm sugar syrup
100g palm sugar
200ml water

tapioca
Place the tapioca in a bowl, cover with cold water and leave to swell overnight. The next day, drain off all excess water through a sieve.

Bruise the lime leaves and lemongrass stalk to release their flavour. Place in a heavy-based saucepan with the coconut milk, lime zest and tapioca and simmer for 10–15 minutes, stirring very frequently as it sticks easily. It is ready when the tapioca pearls are opaque and just tender. Most of the coconut milk should have been absorbed, making it thick and creamy. Remove from the heat, leave to cool, then place in a bowl and chill. When ready to serve, squeeze in the lime juice and mix well.

lychee granita
Cover the gelatine leaf with cold water and soak for about 5 minutes, until soft and pliable. Meanwhile, put the water and sugar in a saucepan and bring to the boil, stirring to dissolve the sugar. Cook for 1 minute, then remove from the heat. Squeeze all the water out of the gelatine, add the gelatine to the syrup and stir until dissolved. Place the lychees and the syrup in a liquidiser and blend to a smooth purée. Pass through a fine sieve and stir in the lime juice.

Place the mixture in a shallow container and freeze for 2–3 hours, until it has started to harden around the sides. Using a fork, push the outside into the middle, then even the surface and replace in the freezer. Repeat after 2 hours and continue until the mixture consists of even ice crystals.

marinated pineapple
Slice the pineapple as thinly as possible; at the restaurant we use a meat slicer but a very sharp knife will do. Place carefully in a bowl, sprinkle with the sugar, then add the lime juice and lemon balm. Cover and leave in the fridge to marinate for 3–4 hours.

palm sugar syrup
Place the palm sugar and water in a saucepan and bring to the boil, stirring to dissolve the sugar. Simmer until reduced by half, then leave to cool.

serving
Remove the granita from the freezer and fork it over again. Divide the tapioca between 6 serving bowls, drizzle with the palm sugar syrup and arrange a layer of pineapple on top, scrunched up neatly. Top with a pile of lychee granita.

poached apricots with violet ice cream and biscuit glacé of olive oil

It may seem a little strange to use olive oil in a dessert but I am not the first to do so by any means, and it does have its merits. I used it in my first book, *Essence* (Absolute Press, 2006) to make a wonderful Pistachio and Olive Oil Cake. For this recipe, the oil adds a wonderful fruitiness – hence this very light and flavoursome version of a *biscuit glacé*, which is like a cross between a parfait and an ice cream. It is up to you to find the best-quality olive oil you can, one with a good fruitiness and low acidity. It goes well with soft fruits such as peaches and nectarines, as well as the apricots. The violet ice cream has a lovely subtle taste that reminds me of a childhood sweet, Parma violets.

Serves 12

for the biscuit glacé
150g caster sugar
50ml water
3 eggs, separated
1½ gelatine leaves
150ml extra virgin olive oil, at room
    temperature
juice of ½ lemon
400ml double cream

for the violet ice cream
750ml milk
375ml double cream
70g fresh violets
9 egg yolks
140g caster sugar
50g violet syrup (available from some
    specialist food shops)

for the poached apricots
200g caster sugar
750ml water
1 vanilla pod, slit open lengthwise
2 strips of lemon zest
25g violet syrup
18 ripe apricots, halved and stoned

biscuit glacé
Place 100g of the caster sugar in a saucepan with the water and bring slowly to the boil, stirring until dissolved. Boil without stirring until the mixture reaches 120°C on a sugar thermometer and is just starting to change colour. Meanwhile, place the egg yolks in a freestanding electric mixer and whisk on high speed until thick and white. When the sugar syrup reaches the correct temperature, pour it on to the egg yolks in a slow, steady stream, whisking all the time. Soak the gelatine in cold water for about 5 minutes, until soft and pliable. Squeeze out all the water and add the gelatine to the egg yolk mixture. Keep whisking until the mixture is cool, then add the olive oil in a steady stream, as if making mayonnaise. Finally add the lemon juice.

In a separate bowl, whisk the egg whites until frothy, then add 25g of caster sugar and whisk to soft peaks. Add the remaining 25g of sugar and beat well.

Whip the cream to a light ribbon stage, allowing a pattern to form and hold its shape but being careful not to overwork it. Fold the cream into the olive oil mixture, then fold in the egg whites. Divide the mixture between 12 dome moulds, about 75ml in capacity, tapping them gently on the worktop to remove any air pockets. Freeze for at least 6 hours.

violet ice cream
Put the milk, cream and violets in a heavy-based saucepan and bring gently to just below the boil. Remove from the heat and leave to infuse for at least 2 hours, preferably overnight.

Gently bring back to the boil. Meanwhile, whisk the egg yolks and sugar together until pale and creamy. Pour half of the milk mixture on to the egg yolks, whisking to combine, then pour this back into the saucepan. Cook over a gentle heat, stirring constantly with a wooden spoon, until the mixture has thickened enough to coat the back of the spoon (it should register about 84°C on a thermometer). Strain immediately through a fine sieve into a large bowl to help stop the cooking. Leave to cool, then stir in the violet syrup. Transfer to an ice-cream machine and freeze according to the manufacturer's instructions. Transfer to the fridge to soften slightly about 10 minutes before serving.

poached apricots
Place all the ingredients except the apricots in a large saucepan and bring slowly to the boil, stirring to dissolve the sugar. Reduce the heat and simmer for 5 minutes. Add the apricot halves and poach gently for 1–2 minutes, then remove from the syrup. When they are cold, return them to the syrup. Chill until ready to serve.

serving
Remove the biscuit glacé from the freezer. Dip the moulds in hot water for 2–3 seconds, then turn out on to serving plates. Allow to stand for 3–4 minutes before serving. Add 3 apricot halves, a little of their syrup and a scoop of violet ice cream to each plate.

lemon meringue tart

One of my favourite classic desserts is lemon meringue pie, but only when it is as fresh as possible – after 5–6 hours the meringue starts to 'weep'. So I came up with this version for the restaurant. It is assembled at the last minute and because of this you have wonderful crisp meringue and very crisp pastry, giving a perfectly clean and refreshing dessert. It is served with angelica and lemon sorbet and jelly, plus some zingy, fresh homemade cardamom yoghurt.

Serves 10

for the tart
1 quantity of Sweet Pastry (see page 19)
250ml lemon juice
grated zest of 3 lemons
600ml double cream
14 egg yolks
125g caster sugar
250g unsalted butter, diced
3 gelatine leaves

for the meringue
30ml liquid glucose
50ml water
125g caster sugar
100g egg whites (about 3)

for the angelica and lemon sorbet
225ml lemon juice
grated zest of 2 lemons
250ml water
25ml liquid glucose
100g caster sugar
100g fresh angelica
1 1/2 gelatine leaves

for the angelica and lemon jelly
200ml lemon juice
150ml water
180g caster sugar
40g fresh angelica leaves
2 gelatine leaves

to serve
200g Cardamom Yoghurt (see page 18)

tart
Roll the pastry out on a lightly floured surface until it is 2mm thick. Cut to a 12 x 36cm rectangle, transfer to a baking sheet and place in the freezer for a few minutes to firm up. Remove from the freezer, prick all over with a fork and cut into 10 rectangles about 3.5 x 12cm. Transfer to a baking tray lined with baking parchment and place in an oven preheated to 160°C/Gas Mark 3 for 5-7 minutes, until golden brown. Remove from the oven and leave to cool. Store in an airtight container until needed.

Bring the lemon juice and zest to the boil in a medium saucepan, reduce the heat and simmer for 2 minutes. Pour in the double cream and bring back to the boil, then remove from the heat. Whisk the egg yolks and caster sugar together and pour on the lemon cream, whisking constantly, then beat in the butter a little at a time. Return the mixture to the pan and put it back on the heat for just a couple of minutes, until finger warm. Soak the gelatine in cold water for about 5 minutes, until soft and pliable. Squeeze out all the water and add the gelatine to the pan, stirring until dissolved. Pass the mixture through a fine sieve into a jug.

Line a 36 x 11.5 x 4cm metal cooking frame with a double layer of cling film with a little overlap. Put the frame in a roasting tin lined with a cloth - this helps protect the lemon mixture from direct heat. Fill the frame to the top with the lemon mixture, then half fill the roasting tin with hot water. Place in an oven preheated to 120°C/Gas Mark 1/2 and bake for 30-40 minutes, until the custard is just set when you shake the tray gently.

Take out of the oven and remove as much water as you can from the roasting tin. Leave to cool in the tin and then place in the fridge in the tin to chill.

meringue
Place the glucose, water and 100g of the caster sugar in a saucepan and bring to the boil, stirring to dissolve the sugar. Cook without stirring until it reaches 120°C on a sugar thermometer. When it reaches 110°C, start whisking the egg whites with the remaining caster sugar in a freestanding electric mixer. When the egg whites have formed soft peaks and the syrup has reached the correct temperature, turn the machine down and slowly pour in the syrup down the side of the bowl in a thin, steady stream. Continue whisking until the meringue is cold.

Place the meringue in a piping bag fitted with a small nozzle and pipe it into 4–5cm spikes flat along a baking sheet lined with baking parchment. Place in an oven preheated to 100°C/Gas Mark 1/4 and bake for 50 minutes-1 hour with the door slightly open. The meringues should be dry and crisp; return them to the oven for longer, if necessary. Leave to cool and then store in an airtight container until needed.

angelica and lemon sorbet
Place the lemon juice, lemon zest, water, glucose and caster sugar in a medium saucepan and bring to the boil, stirring to dissolve the sugar. Remove from the heat, add the angelica leaves and then pour into a liquidiser. Blend until smooth. Soak the gelatine in cold water for about 5 minutes, until soft and pliable. Squeeze out all the water and add the gelatine to the syrup. Stir until dissolved, then pass through a fine sieve. Transfer to an ice-cream machine and freeze according to the manufacturer's instructions. Transfer to the fridge to soften slightly about 10 minutes before serving.

angelica and lemon jelly

Bring the lemon juice, water and caster sugar to the boil in a medium saucepan, stirring to dissolve the sugar. Remove from the heat, add the angelica leaves and place in a liquidiser. Blend until smooth. Soak the gelatine in cold water for about 5 minutes, until soft and pliable. Squeeze out all the water and add the gelatine to the syrup. Stir until dissolved, then pass through a fine sieve into a baking tray to a depth of 1cm. Place in the fridge to set.

serving

Trim the ends of the lemon mixture and cut it into 10 slices the same size as the pieces of pastry. Place directly on to the cooked pastry bases, then top with some pieces of meringue at different angles and flash a blowtorch over them to colour them lightly. Place a few streaks of cardamom yoghurt on each serving plate. Then add the lemon meringue, 2 scoops of sorbet and a couple of small scoops of jelly.

mille feuille of lemon verbena cream with raspberry sorbet and lemon verbena jelly

I wanted to make a dessert including a pastry that was extremely light and quick to make, without all the fuss of puff pastry. So here I have baked filo pastry with sugar and butter to give a very crisp finish. It is layered with lemon verbena cream, which has a delicious lemon sherbet flavour. Lemon balm or mint would be a good substitute. The raspberry sorbet adds that final taste of summer.

Serves 6

for the raspberry sorbet
$3/4$ gelatine leaf
125ml water
125g caster sugar
40ml liquid glucose
500g fresh raspberries
juice of $1/2$ lemon

for the lemon verbena cream
400ml milk
2 eggs
2 egg yolks
150g caster sugar
50g cornflour
100g lemon verbena leaves
100g unsalted butter, diced
$1^1/2$ gelatine leaves
65ml double cream, lightly whipped

for the lemon verbena jelly
250ml lemon juice
150ml water
200g caster sugar
50g lemon verbena leaves
$2^1/2$ gelatine leaves

for the filo wafers
4 sheets of filo pastry
75g unsalted butter, melted
50g icing sugar

for the raspberry garnish
300g fresh raspberries
juice of $1/4$ lemon
10g caster sugar

raspberry sorbet
Soak the gelatine in cold water for about 5 minutes, until soft and pliable. Meanwhile, put the water, sugar and glucose in a pan and bring to the boil, stirring to dissolve the sugar. Remove from the heat. Squeeze out all the water from the softened gelatine and add the gelatine to the sugar syrup. Stir until dissolved, then leave to cool.

Purée the raspberries in a blender with half the syrup. Add the remaining syrup, pulse once and then pass through a fine sieve. Add the lemon juice, transfer the mixture to an ice-cream machine and freeze according to the manufacturer's instructions. Transfer to the fridge to soften slightly about 10 minutes before serving.

lemon verbena cream
Bring the milk to the boil in a medium saucepan and remove from the heat. Whisk the eggs, egg yolks, sugar and cornflour together in a bowl. Gradually add the milk, whisking constantly, then return the mixture to the saucepan. Cook over a medium heat for 4–5 minutes, stirring all the time, until thickened, adding the lemon verbena half way through. Remove from the heat, place to one side to cool a little, then stir in the butter bit by bit until completely melted.

Soak the gelatine in cold water for about 5 minutes, until soft and pliable. Squeeze all the water out of the gelatine and add to the lemon verbena mixture. Stir until dissolved, then place in a liquidiser and blend to a smooth purée. Pass through a fine sieve into a bowl, lay a little cling film on top of the mixture and leave to cool. Fold in the double cream, cover and store in the fridge until needed.

lemon verbena jelly
Put the lemon juice, water and caster sugar in a saucepan and bring to the boil, stirring to dissolve the sugar. Remove from the heat, add the lemon verbena leaves and place in a liquidiser. Blend until smooth. Soak the gelatine in cold water for about 5 minutes, until soft and pliable. Squeeze out all the water and add the gelatine to the syrup. Stir until dissolved, then pass through a fine sieve into a baking tray in a layer 7–8mm deep. Place in the fridge until set, then cut into 7–8mm dice.

filo wafers
Lay 2 sheets of filo pastry on the work surface, brush heavily with melted butter, then dust with icing sugar. Place the remaining sheets on top, brush with the remaining butter and dust with icing sugar. Carefully lift on to 2 lined baking trays. Place a sheet of baking parchment on top, then a heavy baking sheet on top of that. Place in an oven preheated to 200°C/Gas Mark 6 and bake for 5 minutes. Check that the pastry is golden brown, then remove from the oven. Lift off the baking sheets and paper and cut the filo into 36 strips, 1cmx10cm. Place them back on a baking sheet lined with baking parchment. Dust with more icing sugar and return to the oven for 2–3 minutes, watching very carefully. The icing sugar should melt and coat the pastry. Remove from the oven and leave to cool.

raspberry garnish
Pick through the raspberries and reserve the smallest 200g. Place the remainder in a liquidiser with the lemon juice and caster sugar and blend to a smooth purée.

Pass through a fine sieve and store, covered, in the fridge until needed.

serving
Remove the lemon verbena cream from the fridge, beat well, then place in a piping bag. Lay out 24 filo strips on a work surface and pipe the lemon verbena cream in a line down the centre of each one. Place 12 of them on top of the other 12 and then top with the remaining unpiped filo. Dust with icing sugar.

Slash a few streaks of raspberry purée on each plate, carefully add 2 piles of filo at different angles, then a couple of small scoops of raspberry sorbet. Finally arrange the reserved raspberries and the jelly on the plates.

vegetable

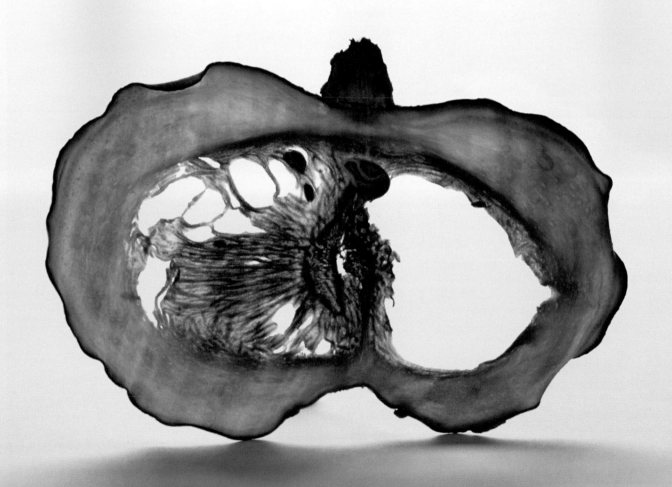

Making desserts out of vegetables is not as unusual as it may seem. They are used in many countries to finish a meal: in the South of France, for example, there are several vegetable-based desserts, such as tourte de blette (made with chard), corn cakes and pumpkin tarts.

Fruit is often added to savoury dishes, so it isn't too much of a jump to switch roles and present vegetables in a sweet dish. It offers the chance to marry different flavours and textures, and to capitalise on the natural sweetness that characterises many vegetables, such as sweetcorn, beetroot, carrots and parsnips. Rhubarb, which is in fact a vegetable, is universally accepted as an ingredient in desserts, while carrot cake is very familiar to everyone, so it's about time a few others were given a chance.

If you don't like a particular flavour in the recipes below, feel free to play with the ingredients – substituting parsnip, beetroot or pumpkin for carrot, for example.

'Fruit is often added to savoury dishes, so it isn't too much of a jump to switch roles and present vegetables in a sweet dish. It offers the chance to marry different flavours and textures, and to capitalise on the natural sweetness that characterises many vegetables, such as sweetcorn, beetroot, carrots and parsnips.'

jerusalem artichoke cheesecake with bergamot glaze and peanut ice cream

Jerusalem artichokes may seem a particularly strange choice for a dessert but they are used without comment in the States, albeit under the name 'sunchokes'. This cheesecake has a wonderfully earthy flavour, which is complemented by the peppery note of bergamot oranges in the glaze. If you can't get them, however, mandarins will work just as well. If you would like to try a different glaze, chicory is good, particularly if you change the ice cream to coffee with mocha undertones. We have also served this cheesecake with Earl Grey tea ice cream and bergamot jelly.

Crosnes, which are caramelised and used as a garnish here, are also known as Japanese artichokes. They are funny-looking things, almost like witchetty grubs, and taste like a cross between artichokes and salsify.

You really have to use Philadelphia cream cheese when making the cheesecake. We've tried other brands and they just don't work.

Serves 8–10

for the cheesecake base
200g Hobnob biscuits
125g unsalted butter, melted

for the cheesecake filling
275g Jerusalem artichokes, peeled
125g Philadelphia cream cheese, at room temperature
15g plain flour
400g mascarpone cheese
3 eggs
2 egg yolks
90g caster sugar
100g white chocolate, melted

for the bergamot glaze
500g bergamot oranges
200g caster sugar
500ml water
3 gelatine leaves
juice of 1 lemon

for the peanut ice cream
150g peanuts, toasted and skinned
500ml milk
200ml double cream
6 egg yolks
100g caster sugar
25ml liquid glucose

for the crosnes
250g crosnes, trimmed
200g caster sugar
50ml water
a pinch of salt
25g unsalted butter

to serve
50g peanuts, toasted and skinned
50g smooth peanut butter, thinned with a little warm water

cheesecake base
Grease and line a deep 20cm loose-based cake tin. Wrap foil around the base and sides to make it watertight.

Place the biscuits in a food processor and grind coarsely. With the machine running, slowly pour in the melted butter. Spread the mixture over the base of the tin in a layer about 5mm thick, pushing it well down, then chill.

cheesecake filling
Steam the Jerusalem artichokes for about 30 minutes, until tender, then purée in a liquidiser or food processor and pass through a fine sieve. Weigh the purée; you will need 150g for the cheesecake.

Mix the cream cheese with the flour. Add the mascarpone, eggs and egg yolks and mix well. Stir in all the other ingredients, including the Jerusalem artichoke purée, then pour the mixture into the prepared tin. Place in a roasting tin and half fill the tin with hot water. Bake in an oven preheated to 90°C (or in a very low gas oven) for about 2 hours, until the filling is set. Remove from the oven, cover with cling film and allow to cool for 1 hour. Uncover, remove from the roasting tin and place in the fridge.

bergamot glaze
Wash the bergamots thoroughly. Place the caster sugar and water in a heavy-based pan and bring slowly to the boil, stirring to dissolve the sugar. Add the bergamots – they should be covered by the syrup. Bring back to the boil and simmer for 50 minutes –1 hour, until the oranges are very soft. If the syrup reduces too much during this process, add a little more water.

Soak the gelatine leaves in cold water for about 5 minutes, until soft and pliable. Place the oranges in a food processor with half the syrup and blend to a purée, adding more syrup if necessary to give the consistency of double cream. Strain through a fine sieve and taste; add enough lemon juice to give a well-flavoured purée. Squeeze all the water out of the gelatine, add the gelatine to the orange mixture and stir to dissolve. Leave the glaze until it is lukewarm, then pour it on top of the cheesecake in a layer about 5mm thick. Return it to the fridge to set.

peanut ice cream
Place the peanuts, milk and cream in a heavy-based saucepan. Gently bring to just below the boil, then remove from the heat and leave to infuse for 2 hours or even overnight. Gently bring to the boil again.

Meanwhile, whisk the egg yolks with the sugar and glucose until pale and creamy. Pour half of the milk mixture on to the egg yolks, whisking to combine, then pour this back into the saucepan. Cook over a gentle heat, stirring all the time, until the mixture thickens enough to coat the back of the spoon (it should read about 84°C on a thermometer).

Remove from the heat and purée in a liquidiser. Immediately strain through a fine sieve into a large bowl to help stop the cooking. When the mixture is cool, pour it into an ice-cream machine and freeze according to the manufacturer's instructions. Transfer to the fridge to soften slightly about 10 minutes before serving.

crosnes
Bring a medium pan of water to the boil, add the crosnes and cook for 3–4 minutes, until just tender. Drain, refresh under cold running water, then drain again. Place on a piece of kitchen paper to dry.

Put the sugar and water in a heavy-based pan and heat gently, stirring until the sugar has dissolved. Raise the heat and cook without stirring until the mixture turns into a deep golden caramel. Immediately remove the pan from the heat, add the crosnes, salt and butter and stir very gently until all the crosnes are coated in the caramel and the butter has melted. As the mixture cools down, the artichokes will start to be individually coated. Tip the mixture on to a lightly oiled tray and leave to cool, pushing the crosnes around to separate them. Set aside until needed.

serving
Dip a knife into hot water to warm it, then cut the cheesecake into 8–10 slices. Scatter a few toasted peanuts and crosnes on each serving plate and drizzle the plates with a little thinned peanut butter. Put the cheesecake on the plates with a scoop of peanut ice cream.

salted chicory parfait with vanilla rice pudding and bitter chocolate sorbet

This is one of those desserts that we had to work at to get right. When we first started serving it, we presented the rice pudding in a disc shape and served a slice of parfait to the left and a quenelle of sorbet to the right. Some customers complained it was too salty, while others said it was perfect.

When we discovered that the people who ate the parfait first were the ones who found it too salty, we changed the presentation so that diners ate through the layers and got a little of everything. Since then we have had nothing but compliments.

Serves 8–10

for the vanilla rice pudding
2 vanilla pods
75g Carnaroli risotto rice
350ml milk
100ml double cream
50g caster sugar
1¹/₂ gelatine leaves
100ml double cream

for the pastry cream
100ml milk
75ml double cream
40g caster sugar
1 egg yolk
5g cornflour

for the rice tuiles
35g egg white (about 1 large)
40g icing sugar
100g rice pudding (see below)

for the salted chicory parfait
200ml double cream
100ml water
150g caster sugar
6 egg yolks
40ml chicory essence
fine salt, to taste

for the bitter chocolate sorbet
750ml water
250ml milk
50g caster sugar
75ml liquid glucose
100g bitter cocoa powder, plus extra for dusting
240g bitter chocolate (64 per cent cocoa solids), chopped

vanilla rice pudding and pastry cream
Slit the vanilla pods open and scrape out the seeds. Place the pods and seeds in a heavy-based saucepan with the rice, milk, double cream and caster sugar. Bring to the boil, stirring constantly, then reduce the heat to a simmer. Cook for about 20 minutes, until the rice is soft and the mixture is thick and creamy. Remove from the heat and set aside 100g of the rice pudding for making the tuiles.

Cover the gelatine leaves with cold water and leave for about 5 minutes, until soft and pliable, then squeeze out all the water and add them to the remaining hot rice pudding. Leave to cool.

While the rice pudding is cooking, make the pastry cream. Bring the milk and cream to the boil in a small saucepan. Meanwhile, put the sugar, egg yolk and cornflour in a bowl and whisk until well combined. Pour on the hot milk and cream, whisking constantly, then return the mixture to the pan and cook over a low heat until thick, stirring well. Put to one side to cool.

Whip the 100ml double cream for the rice pudding until it has thickened enough to leave a ribbon trail on the surface. Place in the fridge.

When the rice pudding and the pastry cream are cool, lightly mix 150g of the pastry cream with the rice pudding and place in the fridge until almost set. Fold in the whipped cream, cover and store in the fridge until ready to use.

rice tuiles
Place the egg white, icing sugar and rice pudding in a food processor and pulse until blended – the mixture should be broken down but still have a little texture. Place in the fridge for 1 hour.

Brush the mixture on to greased baking sheets, in 10 strips about 14 x 3cm. Place in an oven preheated to 150°C/Gas Mark 2 and bake for 4–5 minutes, until golden. Leave to cool, then store in an airtight container until needed.

salted chicory parfait
Whisk the double cream until it is thick enough to leave a ribbon trail on the surface when the whisk is lifted. Cover and place in the fridge until needed.

Put the water and sugar in a small, heavy-based saucepan and heat gently, stirring until the sugar has dissolved. Bring to the boil and cook without stirring until it turns a deep caramel colour.

Meanwhile, whisk the egg yolks in a freestanding electric mixer until thick and pale. As soon as the caramel is ready, pour it on to the egg yolks in a slow, steady stream, whisking constantly, then continue to whisk until the mixture is cold.

Fold in the chicory essence, the double cream and some salt to taste – it should just be a background flavour. Line a 36 x 11.5 x 4cm metal cooking frame with a double layer of cling film, then place it on a baking tray and pour in the mixture. Cover and freeze until set; this will take at least 6 hours.

bitter chocolate sorbet
Place the water, milk, caster sugar and glucose in a heavy-based pan and bring to the boil, stirring to dissolve the sugar. Whisk in the cocoa powder and simmer for 2 minutes, whisking occasionally. Remove from the heat and leave to cool for 2–3 minutes. Put the chocolate into a bowl and pour in the cocoa mixture, whisking until thoroughly incorporated. Strain through a fine sieve, pour into an ice-cream machine and freeze according to the

manufacturer's instructions. Transfer to the fridge to soften slightly about 10 minutes before serving.

serving
Remove the vanilla pods from the rice pudding. Arrange the rice pudding in an oblong, 7–8mm thick, on each serving plate, smoothing it with a palette knife. Top with a slice of salted chicory parfait and then 3 small scoops of sorbet. Finally, add a rice tuile and dust with cocoa powder.

white asparagus crème caramel, white asparagus caramelised with maple syrup

White asparagus is a particular favourite of mine, There is something about the bitterness that really appeals to me. When I decided to experiment with it as a dessert, I hit upon a combination to balance that bitterness. Enter the maple syrup, whose delicious sweetness and musky caramel taste complement this dish perfectly. Do try it; you will be very pleasantly surprised.

Serves 8

for the white asparagus crème caramel
250ml maple syrup
16 white asparagus spears
300ml milk
300ml double cream
2 eggs
4 egg yolks
50g caster sugar

for the white asparagus caramelised with maple syrup
50g unsalted butter
100ml maple syrup

white asparagus crème caramel
Bring the maple syrup to the boil in a medium, heavy-based saucepan and boil until it reaches 160°C on a sugar thermometer. Pour it into 8 lightly oiled dariole moulds, 120ml in capacity, and leave to cool.

Trim each asparagus spear to 12cm long, then set aside; they are for caramelising with maple syrup. Take 150g of the trimmings, chop them up roughly and place in a saucepan with the milk and double cream. Bring to the boil and simmer for 2 minutes, then remove from the heat and leave to infuse for 1 hour. Pass through a fine sieve, discard the trimmings and return the milk and cream mixture to the saucepan. Bring back to the boil, then remove from the heat again.

Whisk the eggs, egg yolks and sugar together in a bowl, then slowly pour on the cream mixture, whisking constantly. Return to the saucepan and heat through gently for 1 minute, stirring all the time; you just need to warm it through rather than cook it. Remove from the heat, strain into a jug and let the bubbles subside.

Place the dariole moulds in a roasting tin with a cloth placed in the bottom to give an even heat. Pour the custard mixture into the moulds, filling them right up to the brim. Pour enough hot water into the roasting tin to come half way up the sides of the moulds, then place the roasting tin in an oven preheated to 120°C/Gas Mark $1/2$. Cook for 40–50 minutes, until just set. Remove from the oven, take the moulds out of the roasting tin and leave to cool. Chill, preferably overnight.

white asparagus caramelised with maple syrup
Blanch the reserved trimmed asparagus spears in a large pan of boiling water for 3 minutes, then drain, refresh in cold running water and drain again. Spread out on a towel to dry.

Shortly before serving, heat the butter in a cast iron frying pan, add the blanched asparagus and cook over a medium heat until beginning to turn golden. Add the maple syrup and cook until the asparagus is a deep golden colour. Carefully remove from the pan.

serving
Stand the dariole moulds in a tray containing boiling water for 30 seconds, then remove from the tray, run a knife around the edge of each mould to loosen the crème caramel and carefully turn out on to serving plates. Serve with the hot caramelised asparagus.

parnsip croustillant with roasted banana ice cream and muscovado sugar syrup

This is an extraordinarily light dessert. The croustillant has a faint taste of banana, which is why I have paired it with banana ice cream. Glazing it lightly with a blowtorch creates a very thin, crisp crust, which makes a great contrast to the mousse.

As with other dishes in this book, you don't necessarily have to stick to the recipe. If you don't like parsnips, you could try chervil tubers (see page 89) or pumpkin – perhaps using some complementary spices. Try serving it with Peanut Ice Cream (see page 72), or a muscovado one. A fruit purée could be used instead of the parsnip purée, as long as it has the same density; raspberries would go very well.

Serves 8

for the parsnip croustillant
420g parsnips, peeled and chopped
300ml milk
6 eggs, separated
30g plain flour
3 gelatine leaves
60g white chocolate, chopped
125g caster sugar
2 tablespoons water
juice of 1/2 lemon
30g icing sugar

for the roasted banana ice cream
4 medium bananas
125g caster sugar
500ml milk
500ml double cream
10 egg yolks
25ml liquid glucose
a pinch of salt
30ml Crème de Banane liqueur

for the muscovado sugar syrup
200g dark muscovado sugar
100ml water
juice of 1/2 lemon

parsnip croustillant

Cook the parsnips in a pan of boiling salted water for about 25 minutes, until tender. Drain well, then purée in a liquidiser and pass through a fine sieve; you will need 300g purée.

Bring the milk to boiling point in a small saucepan. Whisk the egg yolks and flour together in a bowl and gradually pour the milk on to them, whisking all the time. Return the mixture to the pan and cook, stirring, over a medium heat until thick. Meanwhile, soak the gelatine in cold water for about 5 minutes, until soft and pliable, then squeeze out all the water. Remove the pan from the heat and add the softened gelatine, stirring until dissolved. Then beat in the white chocolate. Fold this mixture into the warm parsnip purée and pass through a fine sieve into a bowl. Set aside. Put the caster sugar and water in a heavy-based saucepan and heat gently, stirring to dissolve the sugar. Raise the heat and boil without stirring until the syrup reaches 120°C on a sugar thermometer.

Meanwhile, whisk the egg whites with the lemon juice in a freestanding electric mixer until they form soft peaks. When the sugar syrup reaches the correct temperature, pour it down the side of the bowl on to the egg whites, whisking constantly. Continue to whisk until cold. Carefully fold into the white chocolate mixture.

Grease 8 rings, 7cm in diameter and 4cm high, and cover the bases with cling film. Fill with the mixture, then cover and place in the fridge for 3–4 hours, until set.

roasted banana ice cream

Peel the bananas, cut them in half lengthways and sprinkle with 50g of the sugar. Turn them over in the sugar, then transfer to a buttered baking tray and place in an oven preheated to 180°C/Gas Mark 4. Cook for 20 minutes, turning them over half way through, until they are a good golden brown colour. Remove from the oven and set aside.

Gently bring the milk and cream to the boil in a heavy-based saucepan. Meanwhile, whisk the egg yolks with the glucose, salt and remaining sugar until pale and creamy. Pour half the milk mixture on to the egg yolks, whisking to combine, then pour this back into the saucepan. Cook over a gentle heat, stirring constantly with a wooden spoon, until the mixture thickens enough to coat the back of the spoon (it should register about 84°C on a thermometer). Remove from the heat, place in a liquidiser with the roasted bananas and blend until smooth. Strain through a fine sieve into a large bowl and stir in the Crème de Banane. Place in an ice-cream machine and freeze according to the manufacturer's instructions. Transfer to the fridge to soften slightly about 10 minutes before serving.

muscovado sugar syrup

Place all the ingredients in a saucepan and bring to the boil, stirring to dissolve the sugar. Simmer until a syrup is obtained; it should be the consistency of a thick cordial. If it is too thick, add a little more water; if it is too thin, boil it a little more. Strain through a fine sieve and set aside.

serving

Run a knife around the edge of the parsnip croustillants and carefully remove them from the ring moulds. Dust the tops heavily with the icing sugar. Glaze the surface quickly with a blowtorch to create an even, golden-brown crust. Place on serving plates, add a scoop of banana ice cream and drizzle with the syrup.

sweet potato cake with spiced mascarpone cream

Choose orange-fleshed sweet potatoes for this rather than the white ones; they have less starch and, to my mind, a better flavour. I have served the cake here with a spiced mascarpone cream and some of the accompaniments that are actually in the cake itself. The sweet potato could be replaced with carrot, parsnip, beetroot or even butternut squash, while the soaking syrup could be made with different flavourings. You could also just serve the cake with the mascarpone cream spread on top and sprinkled with cinnamon.

Serves 8–10

for the garnish
220ml water
150g caster sugar
juice of $^1/_4$ lemon
100g sweet potato, peeled and cut into
    5mm dice
50g walnuts
50g green raisins

for the sweet potato cake
50g unsalted butter
2 eggs
200g soft brown sugar
100ml sunflower oil
200g self-raising flour
5g baking powder
300g sweet potatoes, peeled and grated
$^1/_2$ banana, mashed
grated zest of $^1/_2$ orange
75g walnuts, chopped
75g green raisins
icing sugar for dusting

for the spiced mascarpone cream
300g mascarpone cheese
35g icing sugar
1 teaspoon Cointreau
2g ground mixed spice
grated zest of $^1/_2$ orange

garnish
Put the water, sugar and lemon juice into a saucepan and bring to the boil, stirring to dissolve the sugar. Turn the heat down to a simmer, add the diced sweet potato and poach for 2–3 minutes, until just tender. Remove the sweet potato with a slotted spoon and set aside. Add the walnuts and raisins to the pan and simmer for 2 minutes. Remove from the heat and leave to cool. Return the sweet potato to the pan and set aside.

sweet potato cake
Heat the butter in a small frying pan until it starts to turn brown and smells nutty. Leave to cool. Place the eggs in a mixing bowl with the sugar and whisk until pale and thick. Slowly drizzle in the oil and then the butter as if making mayonnaise, whisking all the time. Sift the flour and baking powder together and fold them into the egg mixture. Add all the remaining ingredients except the icing sugar and mix lightly. Transfer the mixture to a greased, lined 30 x 20 x 3cm baking tray and place in an oven preheated to 180°C/Gas Mark 4. Bake for 40 minutes–1 hour, until a knife inserted in the centre comes out clean.

Allow the cake to cool a little, then remove it from the tin, lightly prick it all over and douse with half the syrup from the garnish. Leave to cool completely.

spiced mascarpone cream
Beat all the ingredients together until thick, then chill.

serving
Cut the cake into squares and serve it cold, or put the pieces on a baking sheet and heat them in the oven for 3–4 minutes. Place on serving plates and scatter the garnish around, then add 2 scoops of mascarpone cream to each plate.

Alternatively you could spread the cream on top of the whole cake, then cut it into squares and scatter with the garnish.

swiss chard and confit melon tart

This is based on a classic Swiss chard tart from the South of France, known as *tourte de blette*, which is served as a dessert. Made slightly less sweet, it can also be served as a starter with a side salad. Traditionally it is covered with a pastry lid, making it more of a pie than a tart. My version omits the lid, because I rather like the rustic look of the filling. I have also added some crystallised melon, which seemed logical as the South of France produces superb crystallised fruits. We normally serve this with orange-flavoured crème fraîche but it is good with any citrus fruits or even a crystallised melon ice cream. It makes a perfect finish to a light summer meal.

Serves 12–14

1 quantity of Sweet Pastry (see page 19)
500g Swiss chard leaves (you will need to buy about 1kg leaves and strip out the stalks)
3 eggs
245ml double cream
75g Parmesan cheese, grated
175g soft brown sugar
4 Granny Smith apples, peeled, cored and cut into slices 2–3mm thick
100g green raisins
100g dried figs, chopped
200g crystallised melon, chopped
grated zest of 1 orange
50ml orange flower water
125g pine kernels, lightly toasted
icing sugar for dusting

Roll out the pastry on a lightly floured work surface and use to line a buttered loose-bottomed tart tin, 22cm in diameter and 3–3.5cm deep. Chill for 40–50 minutes, then prick the base with a fork. Line the pastry case with baking parchment and fill with rice or baking beans. Place on a baking sheet in an oven preheated to 180°C/Gas Mark 4 and bake blind for 10–15 minutes, until very lightly coloured. Carefully remove the paper and beans, return the pastry case to the oven for 1–2 minutes to dry out the base, then set to one side.

Bring a large pan of water to the boil. Add the Swiss chard greens and blanch for 1 minute, then drain and refresh in cold water. Drain again and squeeze out as much water as possible. Shred the chard finely and set aside.

Lightly beat the eggs, then add the double cream, Parmesan and sugar and whisk until well combined. Place all the remaining, ingredients except the icing sugar in a bowl with the chard and mix together. Pour on the cream mixture and stir to combine. Place in the pastry case, arranging the ingredients quite rustically. Place in the oven at 180°C/Gas Mark 4 and cook for 30–40 minutes, until the custard is just set. Remove from the oven and leave to cool. Serve dusted with a little icing sugar.

sweetcorn cream with caramel and popcorn ice cream

Every now and then I have a quiet day in and watch some movies. Of course, movies wouldn't be movies without popcorn, and I particularly love the buttered caramel variety sprinkled with a little salt. I decided to make a dessert inspired by this. The sweetcorn cream is rather like a panna cotta and tastes simply lovely. Its subtle flavour goes so well with the other components of this dish.

You will end up with much more popcorn craquant than you need for this recipe, but it will all be eaten, it is just so moreish – and why shouldn't the chef have a few perks!

Serves 10–12

for the popcorn ice cream
50ml sunflower oil
30g popping corn
300ml milk
200ml double cream
5 egg yolks
75g caster sugar
2 teaspoons liquid glucose
30g unsalted butter
a pinch of salt

for the sweetcorn cream
400g fresh sweetcorn from the cob (you will need 3–4 cobs)
400ml milk
250ml double cream
4 egg yolks
50g caster sugar
2¹/₂ gelatine leaves

for the popcorn craquant
75ml sunflower oil
50g popping corn
300g caster sugar
75ml water
75g salted butter

for the caramel
200g caster sugar
25ml water
100ml double cream
100g unsalted butter

popcorn ice cream

Heat the sunflower oil in a large saucepan over a medium heat, add a few kernels of corn and place a lid on the pan. When the corn starts popping, add the rest of the corn kernels and immediately put the lid back on. Shake the pan from side to side occasionally until the corn stops popping. Remove the lid and take the pan off the heat.

Put the milk, cream and popped corn in a heavy-based saucepan, bring gently to just below the boil, then remove from the heat. Leave to infuse for 2 hours. Strain the liquid through a fine sieve into a clean pan, pushing hard to get as much of the juice out of the popcorn as possible. Gently bring to the boil again. Meanwhile, whisk the egg yolks with the sugar and glucose until pale and creamy. Pour half the milk mixture on to the egg yolks, whisking to combine, then pour this back into the saucepan. Cook on a gentle heat, stirring constantly with a wooden spoon, until the mixture thickens enough to coat the back of the spoon (it should register about 84°C on a thermometer). Whisk in the butter, add the salt, then immediately strain through a fine sieve into a large bowl to help stop the cooking. Leave to cool. Place the mixture in an ice-cream machine and freeze according to the manufacturer's instructions. Transfer to the fridge to soften slightly about 10 minutes before serving.

sweetcorn cream

Put the sweetcorn, milk and cream in a large saucepan and bring to the boil. Simmer for 3 minutes, then transfer to a liquidiser and blend until smooth. Whisk the egg yolks and caster sugar together in a bowl, then whisk in the sweetcorn mixture. Return to the saucepan and cook over a medium heat for 2–3 minutes, stirring all the time. Be careful not to let the mixture boil; it should just thicken slightly. Meanwhile, soak the gelatine in cold water for about 5 minutes, until soft and pliable.

Remove the sweetcorn mixture from the heat. Squeeze out all the water from the softened gelatine and whisk the gelatine into the sweetcorn cream, stirring until dissolved. Pass through a fine sieve, pushing as much of the liquid through as possible. Place to one side for the bubbles to subside, then pour into moulds about 120ml in capacity. Leave in the fridge to set for at least 6 hours, preferably overnight.

popcorn craquant

Heat the sunflower oil in a large saucepan over a medium heat, add a few kernels of corn and place a lid on the pan. When the corn starts popping, add the rest of the corn kernels and immediately put the lid back on. Shake the pan from side to side until the corn stops popping. Remove the lid and take the pan off the heat.

Put the sugar and water in a large, heavy-based saucepan and heat gently, stirring to dissolve the sugar. Bring to the boil and cook without stirring until it becomes a deep golden caramel. Remove from the heat and whisk in the butter, being careful as it will splutter. Add the popped corn and stir until it is well coated in the caramel.

Tip the mixture out on to an oiled flat baking tray, spreading it quickly into a single layer. Place a sheet of baking parchment on top and roll it out flat with a rolling pin. Place to one side to set. Break into even pieces and set aside.

Put the sugar and water in a heavy-based pan and heat gently, stirring until the sugar has dissolved. Bring to the boil and cook without stirring until it turns into a rich, deep caramel; be careful not to take it too far or it will be bitter. At the moment you are happy with the colour, remove the pan from the heat and pour in the double cream little by little; be very careful, as it will spit. Whisk gently until the caramel has dissolved. Cool slightly and whisk in the butter, then leave to cool completely.

Dip the sweetcorn creams in hot water for 2–3 seconds, then remove the creams from the moulds and place on serving plates. Place a few slashes of caramel sauce on each plate, add a few pieces of popcorn craquant and finally a scoop of ice cream.

golden beetroot parfait with cheltenham beetroot sorbet and beetroot honeycomb

Beetroot has a very versatile taste – delicious as a savoury, it is equally good as a dessert. I have used two different varieties here: golden beetroot and our very own purple Cheltenham beetroot. They are partnered with an orange curd for a bit of zing, plus beetroot honeycomb to add some texture. This dish would also go very well with a Sichuan pepper ice cream, the mandarin notes of the peppercorns complementing the beetroot.

Serves 8

for the golden beetroot parfait
450g golden beetroot
6 egg yolks
140g caster sugar
grated zest of 1/2 orange
30ml water
250ml double cream, semi-whipped
juice of 1/2 lemon

for the cheltenham beetroot sorbet
600g large Cheltenham beetroot
80ml liquid glucose
100g caster sugar
300ml water
30ml red wine vinegar
1 gelatine leaf

for the beetroot crisps
2 large golden beetroot
300g caster sugar
500ml water
juice of 1 lemon

for the beetroot honeycomb
350g raw beetroot, peeled and then juiced in
  a juice extractor (you will need 150ml juice)
225g caster sugar
100ml liquid glucose
60g honey
7.5g ascorbic acid (available from chemists)
10g bicarbonate of soda

for the orange curd
juice and grated zest of 6 oranges
juice and grated zest of 1 lemon
5 egg yolks
2 teaspoons cornflour
250g caster sugar
250g cold unsalted butter, diced

golden beetroot parfait
Place the beetroot in a saucepan, cover generously with water and bring to the boil. Simmer for 40–50 minutes, until tender, then drain, peel and chop roughly. Blend to a purée in a liquidiser, then pass through a fine sieve; you will need 300g purée for the parfait. Leave to cool and then chill.

In a freestanding electric mixer, beat the egg yolks with 20g of the caster sugar until thick and pale. Put the remaining sugar in a pan with the orange zest and water and bring to the boil, stirring to dissolve the sugar. Raise the heat and boil without stirring until the mixture reaches soft-ball stage (it should register 115°C on a sugar thermometer). Slowly pour this syrup on to the egg yolk mixture, whisking all the time. Continue to whisk until cool. Fold in the beetroot purée and then the double cream. Add the lemon juice to bring out the beetroot flavour. Pour into 6 rings, 6cm diameter and 5cm deep, and freeze until firm.

cheltnenham beetroot sorbet
Cook and purée the beetroot as for the parfait, above. Place the glucose, caster sugar and water in a saucepan and bring to the boil, stirring to dissolve the sugar. Add the beetroot purée and vinegar and bring back to the boil. Meanwhile, soak the gelatine in cold water for about 5 minutes, until soft and pliable.

Remove the beetroot mixture from the heat. Squeeze all the water out of the gelatine, then add the gelatine to the pan and stir until dissolved. Pass the mixture through a fine sieve and leave to cool. Place in an ice-cream machine and freeze according to the manufacturer's instructions. Transfer to the fridge to soften slightly about 10 minutes before serving.

golden beetroot crisps
Wash the beetroot and slice as thinly as possible. We use our meat slicer but a mandoline on its thinnest setting would be fine. You will need 24 slices, but it's best to do about 34 in case some are broken.

Put the sugar, water and lemon juice in a saucepan and bring to the boil, stirring to dissolve the sugar. Boil for 2 minutes to make a light syrup, then remove from the heat and leave to cool. Add the beetroot slices and leave to soak in the syrup for 1 hour.

Remove the beetroot slices from the syrup and arrange them in a single layer on a baking sheet lined with baking parchment, making sure they are not touching each other. Place in an oven preheated to 90°C (or a very low gas oven) and leave to dry out for about 2 hours. Remove one crisp from the oven; it will be a little soft but give it a minute to cool and crisp up. If it is still soft, return to the oven for another hour. Leave to cool, then store in an airtight container until needed.

beetroot honeycomb
Put the beetroot juice in a small saucepan and boil until reduced to 75ml. Remove from the heat and leave to cool.

Put the caster sugar, glucose, honey and reduced beetroot juice in a large, heavy-based pan and bring to the boil, stirring all the time to dissolve the sugar. Whisk in the ascorbic acid, then boil without stirring until the mixture reaches 160°C on a sugar thermometer. Immediately whisk in the bicarbonate of soda, being very careful because the mixture will expand in the pan. As soon as the bicarbonate has been whisked in, pour the mixture on to an oiled baking tray. It will expand on the tray again. Leave to cool, then break into pieces and store in an airtight container.

orange curd

Place the orange juice, orange zest and lemon zest in a saucepan, bring to the boil and simmer until reduced to 200ml. Add the lemon juice.

Whisk the egg yolks, cornflour and sugar together in a bowl until well combined. Gradually pour the juice on to the egg yolks, whisking constantly, then return the mixture to the saucepan. Place on a very low heat and stir in the butter, little by little. Cook very gently, stirring all the time with a wooden spoon, until the mixture begins to thicken. Watch it carefully; if it overheats it could scramble. When the spoon leaves a trail behind it, remove the pan from the heat, strain the curd through a fine sieve and leave to cool. It will thicken as it cools. Cover and store in the fridge.

serving

Turn out the parfaits and cut them into 3 slices per mould, making 18 in all; you will have 2 slices left over. Layer 2 slices of parfait between 3 beetroot crisps. Place a slash of orange curd on each serving plate, then the parfait stacks. Scatter some honeycomb pieces on top and finally add a scoop of beetroot sorbet.

set crown prince pumpkin custard with coffee ice cream and grue de cacao

Anyone familiar with my cooking knows that I have a penchant for the Crown Prince pumpkin, a variety I first came across at Over Farm in Ovington, Gloucestershire. It has a glorious deep orange colour, just the right amount of sweetness, a low water content and very little fibre, making it ideal for desserts.

The combination of the set custard – a sort of cross between custard and panna cotta – the coffee ice cream and the crunchy cocoa bean is heavenly. Other accompaniments worth trying are cinnamon ice cream, or indeed one made with any of the warmer spices, such as cloves, star anise or cardamom. You could even serve a mulled wine ice cream or sorbet.

Serves 6

for the set pumpkin custard
800g Crown Prince pumpkin, quartered
 and seeds removed
400ml milk
200ml double cream
6 egg yolks
75g caster sugar
2¹/₂ gelatine leaves

for the coffee ice cream
300ml milk
300ml double cream
6 egg yolks
75g caster sugar
10g milk powder
10ml liquid glucose
50g ground coffee
30ml coffee liqueur, such as Tia Maria

for the grue de cacao
25g grue de cacao
5g bitter cocoa powder

for the craquant discs
200ml liquid glucose
200g caster sugar
50ml water
100g flaked almonds, toasted until golden

set pumpkin custard
Put the pumpkin pieces on a baking tray and cover tightly with foil. Place in an oven preheated to 200°C/Gas Mark 6 and bake for 40–50 minutes, until soft. Remove from the oven, cut the pumpkin flesh off the skin and push it through a fine sieve while still hot. Set aside.

Grease 6 stainless steel rings, 6cm in diameter and 4cm deep, then wrap some cling film tightly around the bases.

Pour the milk and cream into a large saucepan, bring to the boil and then whisk in the pumpkin purée. Simmer for 3 minutes, then place in a liquidiser and blend until smooth.

Whisk the egg yolks and caster sugar together in a bowl, then whisk in the pumpkin mixture. Return the mixture to the saucepan and cook over a medium heat for 2–3 minutes, stirring all the time. Be careful not to let it boil; the mixture should just thicken slightly. Remove from the heat.

Soak the gelatine in cold water for about 5 minutes, until soft and pliable, then squeeze out all the water. Add the gelatine to the pumpkin cream, stirring until dissolved. Pass through a fine sieve, pushing as much of the liquid through as possible. Place to one side until the bubbles have subsided, then pour into the 6 ring moulds. Leave in the fridge to set for at least 6 hours, preferably overnight.

coffee ice cream
Pour the milk and cream into a heavy-based saucepan and bring gently to the boil. Meanwhile, whisk the egg yolks with the sugar, milk powder and glucose until pale and creamy. Pour half the milk mixture on to the egg yolks, whisking to combine, then pour this back into the saucepan. Cook over a gentle heat, stirring constantly with a wooden spoon, until the mixture thickens enough to coat the back of the spoon (it should register about 84°C on a thermometer). Remove from the heat and stir in the ground coffee, then pour the mixture into a large bowl to help stop the cooking. Leave to infuse for 45 minutes. Strain through a fine sieve and add the coffee liqueur. Freeze in an ice-cream machine according to the manufacturer's instructions. Transfer to the fridge to soften slightly about 10 minutes before serving.

grue de cacao
Grind the grue in a food processor to break it up a little. Add the cocoa powder and pulse the machine, just to mix. Store in a sealed container.

craquant discs
Put the glucose, caster sugar and water in a heavy-based saucepan and heat gently, stirring to dissolve the sugar. Bring to the boil and cook without stirring until it has turned into a golden, amber caramel. Immediately pour on to an oiled baking tray and sprinkle with the almonds. Set to one side until cold and very crisp. Break up the caramel, place in a food processor and pulse to a coarse powder. Store in an airtight container.

Shortly before serving, sprinkle the craquant powder in an even layer on a lined baking tray. Place in an oven preheated to 200°C/Gas Mark 6 until it has melted and formed a single sheet of caramel; this will only take a minute or two, so be very vigilant. Remove from the oven, let it cool and, just before it sets, cut out 6 discs the same diameter as the pumpkin custards, plus 2 extra just in case.

serving
Sprinkle a disc of grue on to each serving plate. Turn out the pumpkin custards on to the grue and place a craquant disc on top, followed by a scoop of ice cream.

red pepper foam with strawberry and red pepper sorbet and mandarin custard

This is one of those dishes where the contrasting flavours of the ingredients have evolved over a matter of months. We started off with a lemon custard, which was fine but it just didn't tie all the other elements together, so we switched to orange, which was very good. Then came the mandarin, which worked perfectly – wonderfully sweet, with an irresistible spicy aroma. We used a plain strawberry sorbet to begin with, which worked well, but I wanted to tie it in more with the red pepper. So we added a little red pepper to the strawberries and now it has evolved into a fantastic marriage of flavours.

Serves 8

for the strawberry and red pepper sorbet
30ml liquid glucose
50g caster sugar
100ml water
$^1/_2$ red pepper, deseeded and chopped
500g ripe strawberries
juice of $^1/_2$ lemon

for the mandarin custard
juice of $^1/_2$ lemon
100ml mandarin juice
grated zest of 4 mandarins
550ml double cream
100ml milk
$2^1/_4$ gelatine leaves
100g caster sugar

for the red pepper compote
100ml water
25g caster sugar
juice of $^1/_4$ lemon
grated zest of 1 mandarin
1 red pepper, peeled, deseeded and finely diced, to yield 100g

for the red pepper foam
5 red peppers
juice and grated zest of 1 mandarin
$1^1/_4$ gelatine leaves

strawberry and red pepper sorbet
Place the glucose, caster sugar, water and red pepper in a saucepan and bring to the boil, stirring to dissolve the sugar. Simmer for 3 minutes, then remove from the heat and leave to cool. Place in a liquidiser with the strawberries and lemon juice and blend until smooth. Pass through a fine sieve, then freeze in an ice-cream machine according to the manufacturer's instructions. Remove from the freezer 5 minutes before needed and place in a piping bag fitted with a large star tube.

mandarin custard
Put the lemon juice, mandarin juice and zest in a saucepan and bring to the boil. Add the double cream and the milk and bring to the boil again. Remove from the heat and leave to infuse for 1 hour. Meanwhile, soak the gelatine in cold water for about 5 minutes, until soft and pliable, then squeeze out all the water.

Place the pan back on the heat, bring almost to the boil, then remove from the heat and add the sugar and gelatine. Whisk until they have dissolved, then strain through a fine sieve, pushing as much of the custard through as you can. Leave to cool, then store in the fridge.

red pepper compote
Place all the ingredients except the red pepper in a small saucepan and bring to the boil, stirring to dissolve the sugar. Add the red pepper, reduce the heat to a simmer and cook for 1 minute. Remove from the heat and leave to cool.

red pepper foam
Place the peppers on a sheet of aluminium foil, fold and seal it, then place on a baking tray. Cook in an oven preheated to 180°C/ Gas Mark 4 for 30 minutes, until completely soft. Remove from the oven and leave until cool enough to handle. Remove the skin and seeds from the peppers; you should have roughly 350g pepper flesh.

Cover the gelatine in cold water and leave to soak for about 5 minutes, until soft and pliable. Put 100ml of the syrup from the red pepper compote in a pan with the mandarin juice and zest and bring to the boil. Remove from the heat. Squeeze all the water out of the softened gelatine, add the gelatine to the pan and stir until dissolved. Place in a liquidiser with the red pepper flesh and blend until smooth. Pass through a fine sieve, leave to cool, then place in an Isi cream whipper (see note below). Charge with 2 gas canisters and leave in the fridge overnight.

serving
Have 8 glasses ready and shake the red pepper foam. Squirt a little into the glasses, add a little of the custard, then sprinkle with a little compote. Finally pipe in a little sorbet. Repeat the layers until the glasses are filled.

note
Isi cream whippers are little stainless steel containers that have a gas cylinder injected into them for making whipped cream. Ferran Adrià, from El Bulli restaurant in Spain, has made these famous for many other uses, including foams and fruit and vegetable mousses, and they are now an essential part of the professional kitchen. They can be obtained from online suppliers, including the ones listed on page 148.

chervil tuber ice cream with lexia raisins and miso and verjus panna cotta

Chervil tubers, which are unrelated to the herb chervil, used to be grown as a crop for cattle but are now being cultivated for human consumption. A good greengrocer should be able to obtain them for you. They are a real favourite of mine, in meat dishes and desserts alike. Their complex honey taste goes well with dried fruits as well as acidic flavours. When using, just think of anything that will be complemented by a honey flavour.

We use the white miso and verjus combination on a lobster starter in the restaurant, and it was this initial dish that made me think the flavours could be turned into a dessert. The white miso has a sweetish, light caramel flavour and the verjus a highly acidic note, combining to make a very pleasant sweet and sour taste. If is worth seeking out Lexia raisins, as they have a delicious caramel and Muscat flavour.

Serves 6-8

for the chervil tuber ice cream
350g chervil tubers, peeled
500ml milk
20g milk powder
100ml double cream
5 egg yolks
75g caster sugar
10ml liquid glucose

for the miso and verjus panna cotta
700ml double cream
100ml milk
250g white miso
110g caster sugar
300ml verjus
3 gelatine leaves

for the lexia raisins
75g Lexia raisins
75g Demerara sugar
100ml verjus
50ml water

chervil tuber ice cream
Cook the chervil tubers in boiling salted water for about 20 minutes, until tender, then drain well. Blend to a purée in a liquidiser, then pass through a fine sieve; you will need 250g purée.

Place the milk, milk powder and cream in a heavy-based saucepan, bring gently to just below the boil, then whisk in the chervil tuber purée. Whisk the egg yolks in a bowl with the sugar and glucose until pale and creamy. Pour half the chervil mixture on to the yolks, whisking to combine, then pour this back into the saucepan. Cook over a gentle heat, stirring all the time, until the mixture thickens enough to coat the back of the spoon (it should register about 84°C on a thermometer). Remove from the heat, push through a fine sieve and leave to cool. Cover and place in the fridge to 'mature' for at least a couple of hours, preferably overnight.

Place the mixture in an ice-cream machine and freeze according to the manufacturer's instructions. Transfer to the fridge to soften slightly about 10 minutes before serving.

miso and verjus panna cotta
Put the cream, milk, white miso and sugar in a heavy-based saucepan and bring gently to the boil. Pull to the side of the stove and leave to infuse for 40 minutes, to extract as much of the miso flavour as you can. Meanwhile boil the verjus in a separate saucepan until reduced to 50ml, then set aside.

Soak the gelatine in cold water for about 5 minutes, until soft and pliable, then squeeze out all the water. Bring the miso mixture back to the boil, remove from the heat again and whisk in the gelatine, making sure it has dissolved. Strain through a fine sieve, add the reduced verjus and leave to cool. Pour into lightly oiled dariole moulds, about 130ml in capacity, then cover and place in the fridge until set.

lexia raisins
Place all the ingredients in a saucepan and bring to the boil. Remove from the heat, cover and leave for about an hour, until the raisins have plumped up. Drain, set the raisins aside, then return the juices to the pan and place it back on the stove. Simmer until the juices form a light syrup, then remove from the heat and return the raisins to the pan. Leave to cool.

serving
Dip the panna cotta moulds in hot water for 2–3 seconds, then gently pull them away from the moulds and quickly turn out on to serving dishes. Place a scoop of ice cream to one side, scatter the raisins around and drizzle with the syrup.

roots, pods, seeds and bark

This section covers some of the most powerful flavourings you can find, including ones that have been used as an antiseptic (cloves), a preservative inhibiting the growth of bacteria (cardamom) and an incense to mask bad smells (ginger). Once they were a very precious commodity, for which wars were fought. Nowadays they are readily available, although some of the more exotic ones are still an outrageous price. Spices provide a link with the rest of the world, helping to give us a taste of foods we have enjoyed abroad. They are also used as medicines and provide useful tools in the herbalist's box.

I have included some seeds in this chapter, such as sesame seeds, wattleseeds and green aniseed. Green aniseed is a particular favourite of mine – its flavour can change with the faintest application of heat or more aggressive roasting and they are wonderful with bitter chocolate, and also with the subtleties of soft fruit and the assertive flavours of citrus fruit.

Also here are roots and bark, with a warmth and flavour that add depth to most autmnal desserts.

Some of the ingredients in this chapter can be hard to obtain, so I have listed some of the suppliers I have been using for years on page 148.

'...some of the most powerful flavourings you can find...'

pandan leaf panna cotta with mastic foam

I love Thai food and am particularly fond of coconut rice in pandan leaf. The leaf has a peculiar toasted rice taste. It is quite powerful and a little goes a long way.

I discovered salep and mastic in Turkey, where they are both traditionally used in ice cream. Salep is an orchid root that is dried and ground to a powder, while mastic is the sundried resin of a tree in the pistachio family. The two of them combine to give a flavour quite unlike anything else. It makes a deliciously light and quite unusual pre-dessert, or a dessert if served in bigger glasses.

Serves 10 as a pre-dessert

for the mastic foam
2g mastic (approximately 1 piece)
50g caster sugar
4g salep
500ml milk
1$^1/_2$ gelatine leaves

for the pandan leaf panna cotta
6g pandan leaves, roughly shredded
550ml double cream
200ml milk
100g caster sugar
2$^1/_4$ gelatine leaves

mastic foam
Using a pestle and mortar, crush the mastic to a powder with the sugar, then add the salep. Bring the milk to the boil in a heavy-based saucepan, whisk in the mastic mixture and continue to whisk for 3–4 minutes while the mixture is simmering. Remove from the heat.

Soak the gelatine in cold water for about 5 minutes, until soft and pliable, then squeeze out all the water and whisk the gelatine into the salep mix. Pass through a fine sieve and leave to cool. Place in an Isi cream whipper (see Note on page 88), filling it two-thirds full, put the top on and place in the fridge for 6 hours. Charge with 2 cartridges and you are ready to go.

pandan leaf panna cotta
Place the pandan leaves, cream, milk and sugar in a heavy-based saucepan, bring slowly to a simmer and cook for a couple of minutes. Meanwhile, soak the gelatine leaves in cold water for about 5 minutes, until soft and pliable.

Place the pandan mixture in a liquidiser and blend until smooth, then pass through a fine sieve. Squeeze all the water out of the gelatine and add to the pandan mixture, stirring until dissolved. Allow the bubbles to subside and then half fill some shot glasses with the pandan cream. Cover and place in the fridge for about 4 hours, until set.

serving
Remove the glasses from the fridge about 30 minutes before needed. Squirt the mastic foam over the panna cotta and serve.

mace junket with lemon myrtle madeleines

This comforting, aromatic pudding is simplicity itself to make. Cold junket served with madeleines just out of the oven – delicious.

Mace is the outside 'cage' of the nutmeg, with a subtler taste. You could replace it with ground cassia bark for a lovely warm flavour. Lemon myrtle has a highly aromatic scent, reminiscent of lemongrass or verbena. Finely chopped lemon balm or grated orange zest would make a good substitute.

Serves 6

for the mace junket
900ml milk
seeds from 1 vanilla pod
1 teaspoon ground mace
20g caster sugar
15ml brandy
2 teaspoons rennet
a blade of mace for grating
soft brown sugar for sprinkling

for the lemon myrtle madeleines
125g unsalted butter
4 eggs
200g caster sugar
25ml double cream
220g plain flour
40g ground almonds
grated zest of 2 lemons
15g dried lemon myrtle
juice of 1 lemon
icing sugar for dusting

mace junket
Put the milk, vanilla seeds, mace and caster sugar in a saucepan and bring slowly up to 98°C. Remove from the heat and stir in the brandy. Add the rennet and stir well, then quickly divide between 6 small glass bowls. Leave, without moving the bowls, for the junket to set and then cover and place in the fridge for 3–4 hours before serving.

lemon myrtle madeleines
Place the butter in a small frying pan over a medium heat and cook until golden brown. Cool quickly and then pour through a fine sieve into a bowl. Set aside.

Place the eggs, sugar and cream in a mixing bowl and whisk until creamy and thick. Mix the flour, ground almonds, lemon zest and lemon myrtle together and rain them into the egg mix, mixing well. Add the melted butter very slowly and then the lemon juice. Place in the fridge for at least 4 hours, or overnight.

Lightly butter and flour 30–32 large madeleine moulds and spoon in the mixture. Bake in an oven preheated to 180°C/Gas Mark 4 for 10 minutes or until the madeleines are risen in the centre and golden brown. Remove from the oven and cool for 2–3 minutes before turning out of the moulds and dusting with icing sugar.

serving
Grate some mace over the top of the junket and sprinkle with soft brown sugar. Serve with the warm lemon myrtle madeleines.

green tea cream with lapsang jelly and milk mousse

This fun little pre-dessert utilises two completely contrasting flavours of tea. Lapsang Souchong has a smoky taste, while the green tea is slightly bitter. The milk mousse mellows them both for a smoother finish. You could use any other perfumed tea, including Earl Grey. The key point here is that the tea must be of good quality for a true flavour.

Serves 8

for the milk mousse
1¹/₂ gelatine leaves
350ml milk
150ml double cream
60g caster sugar

for the green tea cream
250ml double cream
250ml milk
1¹/₂ teaspoons green tea, plus extra for
   sprinkling
5 egg yolks
60g caster sugar

for the Lapsang jelly
1¹/₂ gelatine leaves, softened
250ml water
15g caster sugar
1¹/₂ teaspoons Lapsang Souchong tea

milk mousse
Soak the gelatine in cold water for about 5 minutes, until soft and pliable. Bring the milk, double cream and caster sugar to the boil in a saucepan, stirring to dissolve the sugar, then remove from the heat. Squeeze all the water out of the gelatine and add the gelatine to the pan, stirring until dissolved. Leave to cool. Pass the mixture through a fine sieve and place in an Isi cream whipper (see Note on page 88). Place the lid on it and put in the fridge, injecting one cartridge of gas into it. Allow to set overnight. Remove the cream whipper from the fridge 20 minutes before you need it and give it a good shake before use.

green tea cream
Bring the cream and milk to the boil in a saucepan, then remove from the heat and whisk in the green tea. Leave to infuse for 5 minutes. Strain through a fine sieve, return to the heat and bring back to the boil. Meanwhile, whisk the egg yolks and sugar together. Pour on the cream mixture, whisking all the time, then return the mixture to the saucepan and cook over a low heat for 1 minute, stirring constantly. Strain into a jug and pour into 8 moulds. Place the moulds in a roasting tin and pour enough hot water into the tin to come half way up the sides of the moulds. Place in an oven preheated to 150°C/Gas Mark 2 and bake 15–20 minutes, until the creams are just set. Remove from the roasting tin, leave to cool, then cover and chill.

lapsang jelly
Soak the gelatine in cold water for about 5 minutes, until soft and pliable. Bring the water and caster sugar to the boil in a saucepan, stirring to dissolve the sugar, then remove from the heat. Squeeze all the water out of the gelatine, add the gelatine to the hot water and stir until dissolved. Allow to cool for 2 minutes. Add the Lapsang Souchong tea and leave to infuse for 4 minutes, then pass through a fine sieve, discarding the tea leaves. Leave to cool.

Remove the green tea creams from the fridge and pour a 5mm-thick layer of the Lapsang jelly on top. Place back in the fridge to set.

serving
Remove the moulds from the fridge and squirt the milk mousse on top. Sprinkle with a little green tea and serve.

warm black treacle and spice cake

This is my version of ginger parkin. Lighter than the norm, it nevertheless makes a lovely winter warmer of a dessert. I have chosen to serve it with thick custard and some clotted cream. However, it would also be good with an orange cream, made by mixing some finely grated orange zest and boiled, reduced and cooled orange juice with crème fraîche.

Serves 6–8

for the thick custard
1 vanilla pod
200ml milk
250ml double cream
a pinch of nutmeg
6 egg yolks
1 teaspoon cornflour
30g caster sugar

for the black treacle and spice cake
70g dark soft brown sugar
75g black treacle
75g golden syrup
100g plain flour
100g oats, finely ground
$^1/_2$ teaspoon baking powder
2g ground cinnamon
1g ground cloves
4g ground ginger
$^1/_2$ teaspoon bicarbonate of soda
120g unsalted butter, diced
2 eggs
75g candied ginger, chopped, plus 25ml of the ginger syrup

to serve
icing sugar for dusting
clotted cream

thick custard
Slit the vanilla pod in half lengthwise and scrape out the seeds. Put the seeds and pod in a heavy-based saucepan with the milk, cream and nutmeg and bring to boiling point. Meanwhile, whisk together the egg yolks, cornflour and caster sugar until pale and creamy. Pour the cream mixture on to the egg yolks, whisking constantly, then return to the saucepan. Cook over a low heat, stirring with a wooden spoon, until the custard thickens. It should be fairly thick but be careful that you don't overheat it and scramble the eggs. Pass through a fine sieve and leave to cool.

black treacle and spice cake
Put the soft brown sugar, treacle and golden syrup in a saucepan and bring to the boil, then remove from the heat and leave to cool. Place all the dry ingredients in a bowl, add the butter and rub it in until the mixture resembles breadcrumbs. Mix in the eggs, one at a time, then add the cooled treacle mixture, together with the chopped candied ginger and its syrup. Mix well. Cover and place in the fridge for 2 hours to firm up a little.

Place the mixture in a piping bag and pipe evenly into 6–8 buttered 10cm tart tins, about 3cm deep. Place in an oven preheated to 180°C/Gas Mark 4 and bake for 8–10 minutes, until risen and a deep golden brown. I like to keep them just a little underdone so they are slightly gooey in the centre. Leave in the tins for 1–2 minutes before serving.

serving
Turn the cakes out of their tins, dust with icing sugar and serve with the custard and some clotted cream.

green aniseed beignets

These little beignets are so moreish you will love them. Every country in Europe seems to have its own version, from the *churros* of Spain and the *zeppole* of Italy to the *bugnes*, *merveilles* and even *pets de nonne* (nun's farts) of France.

Here I have added some lemon and green aniseed to give them a wonderful flavour, the lemon cutting the richness that comes from deep-frying. You could sprinkle them with lemon or spice sugar. The dough itself can be flavoured with pretty much anything, from elderflower to acacia or orange zest.

Serves 4–8

50ml milk
10g fresh yeast
75g caster sugar
350g plain flour
1/2 teaspoon baking powder
100g softened unsalted butter, diced
2 eggs
grated zest of 1 lemon
3g green aniseed
2 litres vegetable or sunflower oil
icing sugar for dusting

Heat the milk to just finger warm, then add the yeast with 20g of the sugar and whisk in 25g of the flour. Leave in a warm place for about 15 minutes, until frothy.

Place the remaining flour and the baking powder in the bowl of a freestanding electric mixer and rub in the butter until the mixture resembles breadcrumbs. Mix in the eggs, followed by the yeast mixture, lemon zest and aniseed, and beat for 10 minutes using the K beater. The mixture will eventually leave the side of the bowl. Place in a clean bowl, cover and leave in the fridge overnight.

The next day preheat the oil to 180°C in a deep saucepan. Roll out the dough to 3–4mm thick and cut it into strips 1cm wide and 6–7cm long. Fry in batches for 2–4 minutes, until puffed up and golden, checking the temperature of the oil between batches, Remove the beignets from the fryer with a slotted spoon and place on a tray lined with kitchen paper to absorb any excess oil. Sprinkle with icing sugar, toss to remove the excess, then serve.

three crèmes brûlées: sumac, galangal and coriander seed

I know that many of our customers love the little rose geranium brûlées we serve at the restaurant. I gave the geranium recipe in *Essence* (Absolute Press, 2006) and here is a trio of fragrant brûlées to make a wonderful collection.

Sumac has long been used in the Middle East, and its sour, tangy flavour works extremely well in a brûlée. Galangal, which is common in Thai cooking, is similar to ginger but with a citrussy, more perfumed note. Coriander seeds have lemon and mandarin notes that are both subtle and powerful. I use them in all sorts of desserts, including ice creams and bitter chocolate.

These brûlées all have a faint citrus flavour running through them as a common thread, which is why I serve them together here. However, you could serve just a single kind as a pre-dessert.

Serves 8

for the sumac brûlée
25ml lemon juice
10g sumac, ground in a mortar
250ml double cream
1 egg
4 egg yolks
65g caster sugar, plus extra to glaze

for the galangal brûlée
75ml lemon juice
grated zest of 1 lemon
8 slices of galangal, bruised in a mortar
200ml double cream
1 egg
4 egg yolks
65g caster sugar, plus extra to glaze

for the coriander seed brûlée
5g coriander seeds
25ml lemon juice
grated zest of 1 orange
250ml double cream
1 egg
4 egg yolks
65g caster sugar, plus extra to glaze

to serve
icing sugar

sumac brûlée

Put the lemon juice and sumac in a medium saucepan and bring to the boil. Remove from the heat and leave to infuse for 1 hour, then place back on the heat, add the double cream and bring to the boil again. Meanwhile, whisk the egg, egg yolks and sugar together until pale. Pour the cream mixture on to the eggs, whisking all the time, then pour back into the saucepan. Cook over a low heat, stirring constantly with a wooden spoon, until thick (it should reach about 84°C on a thermometer). Be careful not to let it boil or it will scramble. Remove from the heat and strain through a fine sieve, pushing on the sumac to extract as much flavour as possible. Pour into 8 small ramekins and leave to cool, then chill. Sprinkle with a thin layer of caster sugar and glaze the tops with a blowtorch. Leave to cool.

galangal brûlée

Put the lemon juice, lemon zest and galangal in a medium saucepan and bring to the boil. Remove from the heat and leave to infuse for 1 hour, then place back on the heat, add the double cream and bring to the boil again. Meanwhile, whisk the egg, egg yolks and sugar together until pale. Pour the cream mixture on to the eggs, whisking all the time, then pour back into the saucepan. Cook over a low heat, stirring constantly with a wooden spoon, until thick (it should reach about 84°C on a thermometer). Be careful not to let it boil

or it will scramble. Remove from the heat and strain through a fine sieve, pushing on the galangal to extract as much flavour as possible. Pour into 8 small ramekins and leave to cool, then chill. Sprinkle with a thin layer of caster sugar and glaze the tops with a blowtorch. Leave to cool.

coriander seed brûlée

Place the coriander seeds in a small frying pan and dry roast over a medium heat for 2 minutes. Remove from the heat and crush in a mortar. Place in a medium saucepan with the lemon juice and orange zest and bring to the boil. Remove from the heat and leave to infuse for 1 hour, then place back on the heat, add the double cream and bring to the boil again.

Meanwhile, whisk the egg, egg yolks and sugar together until pale. Pour the cream mixture on to the eggs, whisking all the time, then pour back into the saucepan. Cook over a low heat, stirring constantly with a wooden spoon, until thick (it should reach about 84°C on a thermometer). Be careful not to let it boil or it will scramble. Remove from the heat and strain through a fine sieve, pushing on the coriander to extract as much flavour as possible. Pour into 8 small ramekins and leave to cool, then chill. Sprinkle with a thin layer of caster sugar and glaze the tops with a blowtorch. Leave to cool.

serving

Dust the brûlées with icing sugar immediately before serving, then arrange them on 8 serving plates.

crème catalan

This recipe differs slightly from the traditional one because it includes saffron, which gives it a beautiful golden-yellow hue and a truly luxurious flavour. The aroma of the citrus zests lifts the cream to a new dimension, while Maury syrup adds a slight raisin taste.

Serves 8

50g Demerara sugar
450ml double cream
150ml milk
7–8cm piece of cinnamon stick
10g fennel seeds, crushed
a pinch of saffron
1 vanilla pod, slit open lengthwise
grated zest of $^1/_2$ orange
grated zest of 1 lemon
8 egg yolks
65g caster sugar
Maury Syrup (see page 17), for drizzling.

Spread the Demerara sugar out on a flat baking tray and put it in an oven preheated to 120°C/Gas Mark $^1/_2$ for 10 minutes, to get rid of a little of the moisture. Leave to cool, then grind to a powder in a food processor. Store in a sealed jar.

Put the cream and milk in a medium saucepan with all the spices, the split vanilla pod and the orange and lemon zest and bring to the boil. Remove from the heat and allow to infuse for 30 minutes. Put back on the heat and return to the boil. Meanwhile, beat together the egg yolks and caster sugar until pale. Pour the cream mixture on to the egg yolks, mixing constantly, then return it to the pan. Cook over a low heat for 3 minutes, stirring all the time, then push the mixture through a fine sieve.

Wrap cling film around the bases of 8 metal rings, 6.5cm in diameter and 5cm deep, making sure it comes half way up the sides of each one. Place them in a roasting tin with a cloth in the bottom to stop the mixture overheating and scrambling. Pour in the cream mixture, then pour enough boiling water into the tin to come a third of the way up the sides of the rings. Place in an oven preheated to 110°C/ Gas Mark $^1/_4$ and cook for 30–40 minutes, until just set; the cream should wobble ever so slightly when shook.

Remove from the oven and cover the whole tray with cling film so no air escapes. Leave for 30 minutes, then remove the cling film, carefully pour off the water and place the tray in the fridge. Leave for at least 3 hours, preferably overnight, until set.

serving
Remove the cling film from the moulds and place them on 8 serving plates. Sprinkle with the powdered Demerara sugar and glaze evenly with a blowtorch until golden, being careful not to let the plates get too hot. Run a small kitchen knife around the inside of the rings and carefully lift them off. Leave to cool, then drizzle with Maury syrup.

You could turn the moulds out on top of some raspberries and then glaze them, if you like.

liquorice macaroons with tangerine jelly and sorbet

I think liquorice must be my favourite spice. From a very young age, I was given the root to chew on instead of sweets by my aunt and the taste has stayed with me. I use it a lot, not only in desserts but in savoury dishes too. It goes extremely well with pineapple and with citrus fruits – pink grapefruit, lemon and, of course, anything with an orange bias to it. Here it is paired with tangerine jelly and sorbet.

Serves 8

for the tangerine sorbet
2 gelatine leaves
300g caster sugar
300ml water
100ml liquid glucose
1 litre tangerine juice
juice of $^1/_2$ lemon

for the tangerine jelly
1 litre tangerine juice
4 gelatine leaves
200g caster sugar
100ml water
juice of $^1/_2$ lemon

for the liquorice macaroons
200g caster sugar
50ml water
140g egg whites (4-5 whites)
200g icing sugar
200g ground almonds
10g ground liquorice root

for the caramel chocolate ganache
150g caster sugar
30ml water
100ml double cream
150g bitter chocolate (71 per cent cocoa solids), finely chopped

tangerine sorbet
Cover the gelatine with cold water and leave for about 5 minutes, until soft and pliable. Bring the sugar, water and glucose to the boil in a small saucepan, stirring to dissolve the sugar, then pull to one side of the stove. Squeeze all the water out of the gelatine and add the gelatine to the saucepan, stirring until dissolved. Cool and add to the tangerine juice. Stir in the lemon juice, then cover and leave in the fridge overnight. The next day, strain the mixture through a fine sieve, place in an ice-cream machine and freeze according to the manufacturer's instructions. Transfer to the fridge to soften slightly about 10 minutes before serving.

tangerine jelly
Place half the tangerine juice in a saucepan, bring to the boil and simmer until reduced to 50ml. Meanwhile, soak the gelatine in cold water for about 5 minutes, until soft and pliable. Remove the reduced tangerine juice from the heat. Squeeze all the water out of the gelatine and add the gelatine to the pan, stirring until dissolved. Add the sugar and stir to dissolve, then add the remaining tangerine juice, plus the water and lemon juice. Pass through a fine sieve into a bowl and leave to cool. Cover and chill until set; overnight is best.

liquorice macaroons
Put the caster sugar and water in a heavy-based pan and heat gently, stirring to dissolve the sugar. Raise the heat, bring to the boil and cook without stirring until the syrup reaches 120°C on a sugar thermometer. When it reaches approximately 110°C, whisk the egg whites to soft peaks in a freestanding electric mixer. When the syrup reaches the correct temperature, slowly pour it on to the whites, whisking constantly. Carry on whisking until the mixture is thick and very stiff.

Mix the icing sugar and ground almonds together and add slowly to the egg whites, gently folding them in. Finally fold in the ground liquorice root. Place in a piping bag and pipe on to a tray lined with baking parchment, making rounds 5–6cm in diameter; you will need 24. Allow to dry for about 30 minutes. This is important, as it allows a skin to form before you bake them. Place in an oven preheated to 180°C/ Gas Mark 4 and bake for 8–12 minutes. Ideally the vent of the oven should be open, but you could just prop the door open slightly. The macaroons should be firm to the touch and crisp when cool. Remove from the oven, leave to cool, and then remove from the baking parchment.

caramel chocolate ganache
Place the sugar and water in a heavy-based saucepan and heat gently, stirring to dissolve the sugar. Raise the heat, bring to the boil and cook without stirring until the syrup turns into a deep golden caramel. Add the double cream carefully, as it will spit. Bring back to the boil and remove from the heat. Allow to cool for 1–2 minutes.

Put the chocolate in a bowl, pour on the caramel and mix until the chocolate has melted. Leave until completely cold, then whisk a little until smooth.

Serving
Sandwich the macaroons together with the caramel chocolate ganache to make 12. Cut 4 of the macaroons in half and place $1^1/_2$ on each serving plate. Add a few small spoonfuls of tangerine jelly and a scoop of tangerine sorbet.

cinnamon-spiced doughnuts with cinnamon milk purée and chicory and cinnamon milk

Everyone loves doughnuts and these are spiced up a little with cinnamon. You can choose from a multitude of other spices, with cardamom being particularly good.

Serving doughnuts with a glass of milk isn't anything new – Americans have enjoyed the combination for years. I have flavoured the milk with cinnamon, however, which is echoed in the purée and the dusting on the doughnuts, plus some chicory to give it a more luxurious flavour.

Serves 12

for the cinnamon-spiced doughnuts
125ml buttermilk
5g fresh yeast
80g caster sugar
375g plain flour
a good pinch of ground cinnamon
a pinch of salt
1 egg
30ml orange flower water
80g unsalted butter, melted
2 litres vegetable or sunflower oil

for dusting
200g caster sugar
1 teaspoon ground cinnamon

for the cinnamon milk purée
700ml milk
300ml double cream
20g caster sugar
2g carrageen powder
3–4g freshly ground cinnamon (to taste)

for the chicory and cinnamon milk
900ml milk
200ml double cream
1 teaspoon ground cinnamon
20ml chicory essence (Camp coffee)

4 egg yolks
50g caster sugar

cinnamon-spiced doughnuts
Set aside 5ml of the buttermilk. Heat the rest of the buttermilk until finger warm, then add the yeast and good pinch of the sugar. Mix well and set aside in a warm place for about 15 minutes, until frothy.

Place the remaining caster sugar in the bowl of a freestanding electric mixer with the flour, cinnamon and salt. In a separate bowl, mix the egg with the reserved 5ml of buttermilk and the orange flower water. Add the melted butter and the yeast mixture and stir well. Pour into the flour mixture and beat for 10 minutes with the K beater. The dough will eventually leave the side of the bowl. Place in a clean bowl, cover and refrigerate overnight.

Remove the dough from the fridge and divide into cherry-sized pieces. Lightly roll with flour-dusted hands and place on a flour-dusted tray, leaving a little space between each one. Cover and leave in a warm place for about 30 minutes, until doubled in size

Heat the oil to 170°C in a deep-fat fryer or a deep saucepan. Gently drop the doughnuts into the oil, cooking them in 3 or 4 batches, and fry for 1–2 minutes on each side until golden. Remove with a slotted spoon and place on a plate lined with kitchen paper to absorb excess oil. Mix together the caster sugar and cinnamon for dusting and toss the doughnuts in it whilst still warm.

cinnamon milk purée
Put the milk and double cream in a large, heavy-based saucepan, bring to the boil and simmer until reduced to 350ml, being careful it doesn't catch on the bottom of the pan. Remove from the heat.

Mix the caster sugar with the carrageen and cinnamon and whisk it into the reduced milk mixture. Allow to swell for 2–3 minutes, then bring to the boil again, whisking constantly. Remove from the heat, pass through a sieve into a container and leave to cool. Chill for about 4 hours, until set, then purée in a liquidiser until the consistency of clotted cream. Cover and store in the fridge until needed.

chicory and cinnamon milk
Put the milk and cream in a saucepan and bring to the boil. Whisk in the cinnamon and chicory essence and remove from the heat.

Whisk the egg yolks and sugar together in a bowl, then pour on the hot milk, whisking all the time. Return to the saucepan and cook over a low heat, stirring constantly with a wooden spoon, until lightly thickened (it should register about 84°C on a thermometer). Remove from the heat and pass though a fine sieve. Cool and then chill.

serving
Remove the chicory and cinnamon milk from the fridge and froth it up with a blender. Place a slash of cinnamon milk purée on each serving plate, arrange 3 doughnuts on the purée, and add a glass of the chicory and cinnamon milk. Serve the remaining doughnuts in a small bread basket.

star anise and muscovado parfait with bergamot cream and parkin purée

A very complex dish with lots of different flavours, but they all come together to create a wonderful dessert. The citrus tang of bergamot oranges, with their light pepperiness and Earl Grey overtones, contrasts with the bold flavours of muscovado sugar and star anise. The parkin purée includes all the flavours that go into making traditional ginger parkin except the oatmeal. A truly satisfying dessert. If you can't find bergamot oranges, use mandarins instead.

Serves 8

for the star anise and muscovado parfait
100g Spiced Bread (see page 20), made into crumbs in a food processor
405g muscovado sugar
2 star anise, ground
100ml water
6 egg yolks
1 gelatine leaf
200ml double cream, lightly whipped

for the mandarin jelly
1 litre mandarin juice
4 gelatine leaves
200g caster sugar
100ml water
juice of 1/2 lemon

for the parkin purée
450g muscovado sugar
500ml water
juice of 1 lemon
75ml orange juice
10g finely grated orange zest
30g black treacle
100g ginger syrup from a jar of candied ginger
9g agar agar

for the bergamot cream
juice and grated zest of 2 bergamot oranges
400ml milk
175ml double cream
2 eggs
1 egg yolk
75g caster sugar
50g cornflour
1 1/4 gelatine leaves
100g unsalted butter, diced

for the caramel craquant
200ml liquid glucose
200g caster sugar
50ml water
100g flaked almonds, toasted until golden

star anise and muscovado parfait
Sprinkle the crumbs over a baking sheet lined with baking parchment and place in an oven preheated to 150°C/Gas Mark 2 for 10–15 minutes, until they feel coarse. Remove from the oven and leave to cool, then separate the crumbs.

Place 400g of the muscovado sugar in a heavy-based pan with the star anise and water and heat gently, stirring to dissolve the sugar. Raise the heat, bring to the boil and cook without stirring until the syrup reaches 120°C on a sugar thermometer. Meanwhile, in a freestanding electric mixer, whisk the egg yolks with the remaining 5g sugar until thick, airy and pale. Soak the gelatine in cold water for about 5 minutes, until soft and pliable.

When the muscovado sugar syrup reaches the correct temperature, slowly drizzle it on to the egg yolks, with the machine running on high. Squeeze all the water out of the gelatine and add it to the mix while it is still hot. Carry on whisking until cold. Fold in the whipped cream.

Using cling film, tightly cover the base and sides of 8 ring moulds, 5cm in diameter and 5cm deep. Put the parfait mixture in the moulds and place in the freezer for at least 6 hours, preferably overnight.

mandarin jelly
Put half the mandarin juice in a saucepan, bring to the boil and simmer until reduced to 50ml. Meanwhile, soak the gelatine in cold water for about 5 minutes, until soft and pliable. Remove the reduced mandarin juice from the heat. Squeeze all the water out of the gelatine and add the gelatine to the pan, stirring until dissolved. Add the sugar and stir until dissolved, then add the remaining mandarin juice, plus the water and lemon juice. Pass through a fine sieve into a bowl and leave to cool. Cover and chill until set; overnight is best.

parkin purée
Place all the ingredients except the agar agar in a saucepan and bring to the boil, stirring to dissolve the sugar. Reduce the heat to a simmer and cook for 5 minutes. Pull off the stove and add the agar agar. Allow to swell, then place the pan back on the heat and cook for 1 minute, stirring all the time, until it has dissolved. Pass the mixture through a fine sieve into a container, leave to cool and then place in the fridge overnight.

On removing it from the fridge, you will notice that it has set solid. Don't worry; just put it in a liquidiser and blend until completely smooth, scraping the sides down occasionally. Cover and store in the fridge until needed.

(continued on page 108)

(continued from page 106)

bergamot cream

Place the bergamot juice and zest in a saucepan and bring to the boil. Simmer for 3-4 minutes, then add the milk and 50ml of the double cream and bring back to the boil. Whisk the eggs, egg yolk, sugar and cornflour together in a bowl. Add the milk mixture, whisking constantly, then pour the mixture back into the saucepan, place on a medium heat and cook for 4–5 minutes, stirring all the time, until thickened. Meanwhile, soak the gelatine in cold water for about 5 minutes, until soft and pliable.

Remove the pan from the heat, cool slightly, then stir in the butter bit by bit until melted. Squeeze all the water out of the gelatine and add the gelatine to the pan, stirring until dissolved. Pass through a fine sieve into a bowl, lay a little cling film on top of the mixture and leave to cool.

Whip the remaining double cream until it thickens enough to leave a ribbon on the surface, then fold it into the mixture. Cover and store in the fridge until needed.

caramel craquant

Put the glucose, caster sugar and water in a heavy-based saucepan and heat gently, stirring to dissolve the sugar. Bring to the boil and cook without stirring until the syrup has turned into a golden amber caramel. Immediately pour on to an oiled baking tray and sprinkle with the almonds. Set to one side until cold and very crisp. Break up the caramel, place in a food processor and pulse to a coarse powder. Store in an airtight container.

Shortly before serving, sprinkle the craquant powder over a lined baking tray in an even layer. Place in an oven preheated to 200°C/Gas Mark 6 until it has melted and formed a single sheet of caramel; it will only take a minute or two, so be very vigilant. Remove from the oven, let it cool and, just before it sets, cut it into rectangles measuring 8 x 6cm. You will need 16 but do 20 to be safe. Leave to cool and then store in an airtight container with baking parchment between the layers.

serving

Put the bergamot cream in a piping bag and pipe 9 dots of it on to each serving plate, making a rectangle the same size as the craquant rectangles. Place a piece of crquant on top and pipe on top of this the same number of dots. Finish with another piece of craquant. Place a couple of slashes of the parkin purée on the plate, plus a couple of little spoonfuls of the mandarin jelly. Remove the parfait from the freezer and unmould it. Sprinkle some spiced breadcrumbs on top and place on the plates.

wattleseed cream with caramel ice cream and filo wafers

Wattleseed comes from an Australian acacia tree. Roasted and ground, they have flavours of chocolate, caramel, hazelnuts and maybe a little coffee. They are therefore well worth pairing with any of these flavours, and then logically with any of the flavours that match them. They also go well with vanilla and just by themselves in a cream dessert. Here I have paired them with caramel, plus filo wafers for a different texture. The wafers could have ground spices such as cardamom or coriander sprinkled between the layers.

Serves 8

for the caramel ice cream
250g granulated sugar
50ml water
300ml double cream
300ml milk
5g wattleseeds
5 egg yolks
juice of 1/2 lemon

for the wattleseed cream
15g wattleseeds, plus 5g to decorate
650ml double cream
150ml milk
110g caster sugar
3 gelatine leaves

for the caramel
250g granulated sugar
25ml water
100ml double cream
150g unsalted butter, diced

for the filo wafers
6 sheets of filo pastry
100g unsalted butter, melted
50g icing sugar

caramel ice cream
Put the sugar and water in a heavy-based saucepan and heat gently, stirring to dissolve the sugar. Raise the heat, bring to the boil and cook without stirring until it turns into a deep golden caramel. Remove from the heat and immediately pour in the cream little by little, taking care as it will spit. Place back on the stove, add the milk and wattleseeds and stir until the caramel has dissolved. Bring to the boil.

Meanwhile, whisk the egg yolks until pale and creamy. Pour half the caramel milk on to the egg yolks, whisking to combine, then pour this back into the saucepan. Cook over a gentle heat, stirring all the time with a wooden spoon, until the mixture has thickened enough to coat the back of the spoon (it should register about 84°C on a thermometer). Strain immediately through a fine sieve into a large bowl to help stop the cooking. Place in an ice-cream machine and freeze according to the manufacturer's instructions. Transfer to the fridge about 10 minutes before serving.

wattleseed cream
Place a small frying pan over a medium heat, add the 15g wattleseeds and cook until they start popping. Immediately remove from the pan and place in a heavy-based saucepan. Add the cream, milk and sugar and bring gently to the boil. Pull to the side of the stove and leave to infuse for 2 hours.

Cover the gelatine in cold water and leave for about 5 minutes, until soft and pliable, then squeeze out all the water. Bring the wattleseed mixture back to the boil, remove from the heat and whisk in the gelatine, making sure it has dissolved. Strain the mixture through a coarse sieve and leave to cool. Pour it into 8 lightly oiled dariole moulds, about 100ml in capacity, then cover and leave in the fridge.

caramel
Put the sugar and water in a heavy-based saucepan and heat gently, stirring to dissolve the sugar. Raise the heat, bring to the boil and cook without stirring until it turns into a deep golden caramel, being careful not to take it too far or it will be bitter. The moment you are happy with the colour, remove from the heat and pour in the double cream little by little; take care, as it will spit. Whisk until the caramel has dissolved. Cool slightly and then whisk in the butter a little at a time. Leave to cool completely.

filo wafers
Lay 2 sheets of filo pastry on a work surface, brush heavily with melted butter and dust with icing sugar. Place another sheet on top of each one and repeat with the butter and icing sugar. Repeat with the remaining filo, butter and icing sugar. Carefully lift the filo on to 2 baking trays lined with baking parchment. Place a sheet of baking parchment on top, then a heavy baking sheet on top of that. Place in an oven preheated to 200°C/Gas Mark 6 and cook for 5 minutes, until golden brown.

Remove from the oven, remove the trays and paper and cut the pastry into 24 rectangles, 3 x 5cm. Return them to a lined baking sheet, dust with more icing sugar and place in the oven for 2–3 minutes, watching very carefully, just until the icing sugar melts and coats the pastry. Remove from the oven and leave to cool.

serving
Dip the wattleseed cream moulds in hot water for 2–3 seconds, then gently pull the creams away from the edge of the moulds and quickly turn out on to 8 serving dishes. Sprinkle with a little wattleseed. Place a few slashes of caramel on each plate, then a scoop of caramel ice cream. Place a little caramel between the wafers and stand them up.

sesame cannelloni of orange and burdock, with cherries poached in burdock syrup

This simple and fairly quick dessert has some lovely flavours and textures. Crisp and soft, sweet and sour, light and deep – all of these things come into play when eating. The sesame seeds in the caramel give that special toasted flavour that you get at Chinese restaurants.

Poppy seeds or wattleseeds could be substituted for the sesame seeds, while liquorice, star anise or cinnamon could replace the burdock. A rose cream or lemon cream might be nice here.

Serves 6

for the cherries poached in burdock syrup
100g caster sugar
400ml red wine
100ml port
6 lemon verbena leaves
15g dried burdock root, crushed
grated zest of 1 orange
500g cherries, pitted but with the stalks left on

for the orange and burdock cream
40g dried burdock root, crushed
100ml orange juice
grated zest of 1 orange
200ml milk
225ml double cream
2 eggs
2 egg yolks
150g caster sugar
50g cornflour
2 gelatine leaves
100g unsalted butter

for the sesame cannelloni
200ml liquid glucose
200g caster sugar
50ml water
50g sesame seeds
50g flaked almonds, toasted until golden

to serve
24 small lemon verbena leaves

cherries poached in burdock syrup
Put all the ingredients except the cherries in a pan and bring to the boil, stirring to dissolve the sugar. Simmer for 3–4 minutes, then add the cherries and cook for 4–5 minutes longer. Immediately remove the cherries with a slotted spoon, place in a bowl and leave to cool. Simmer the cooking juices until reduced by half and leave to cool. Strain the juices on to the cherries and leave to macerate overnight.

orange and burdock cream
Place the burdock, orange juice and zest in a saucepan, bring to the boil and simmer for 3 minutes. Add the milk and 100ml of the double cream, bring back to the boil, then remove from the heat and set aside for 2 hours to infuse.

Bring the mixture back to the boil. Meanwhile, whisk the eggs, egg yolks, sugar and cornflour together in a bowl. Add the milk mixture, whisking constantly, then pour the mixture back into the saucepan, place on a medium heat and cook for 4–5 minutes, stirring all the time, until thickened. Soak the gelatine in cold water for about 5 minutes, until soft and pliable.

Remove the pan from the heat, cool slightly, then stir in the butter bit by bit until melted. Squeeze all the water out of the gelatine and add the gelatine to the pan, stirring until dissolved. Pass through a fine sieve into a bowl, lay a little cling film on top of the mixture and leave to cool.

Whip the remaining double cream until it thickens enough to leave a ribbon on the surface, then fold it into the mixture. Cover and store in the fridge until needed.

sesame cannelloni
Put the glucose, caster sugar and water in a heavy-based saucepan and heat gently, stirring to dissolve the sugar. Bring to the boil and cook without stirring until it has turned into a golden amber caramel. Immediately pour on to an oiled baking tray and sprinkle with the sesame seeds and almonds. Set to one side until cold and very crisp. Break up the caramel, place in a food processor and pulse to a coarse powder. Store in an airtight container.

Shortly before serving, sprinkle the craquant powder over a lined baking tray in an even layer. Place in an oven preheated to 200°C/ Gas Mark 6 until it has melted and formed a single sheet of caramel; it will only take a minute or two, so be very vigilant. Remove from the oven, let it cool and, just before it sets, cut it into 18 rectangles measuring 12 x 5cm, cutting through the paper too. Place back on a baking sheet on the paper and flash through the oven just to soften. Remove from the oven and wrap each rectangle around some dowling, about 4.5cm in diameter, using the paper to guide it. Leave until set, then slide the cannelloni off the dowling. Keep in an airtight container until needed.

serving
Beat the orange and burdock cream well, place it in a piping bag and pipe into the sesame cannelloni. Place 2 on each plate, side by side, then put a third on top, at an angle. Put the cherries on one side, pour round a little of the syrup, then decorate with the lemon verbena.

wild

I am lucky enough to live near wonderful countryside that supplies us with a great variety of wild foods. Their novel flavours and textures really excite my imagination. Fruits, nuts, roots, leaves and blossoms – they are all there ready for us to use.

I was first introduced to wild food by my Aunt Pat when I was a young boy. She was an extremely gifted hedgerow cook and used to take me on walks down country lanes, pointing, tasting, teaching – something for which I am so grateful now.

In this chapter I have focused on the more readily available wild foods, from sharp-tasting rowan berries to delicious sweet brambles, from acidic, lemony sorrel to gorse flowers with their gentle coconut flavour. And not forgetting elder bushes, which provide us with two very different ingredients: the elderflower, with its soft, gently floral notes, and the deep, powerfully flavoured elderberry. You see, nature has it all.

I am lucky enough to live near wonderful countryside that supplies us with a great variety of wild foods. Their novel flavours and textures really excite my imagination. Fruits, nuts, roots, leaves and blossoms – they are all there ready for us to use.

elderflower mousse with roasted red gooseberries

We know that summer is well and truly here when we see our first red gooseberries. Unfortunately the season is shorter than that of the more common green varieties but that just makes them even more special. They have a sweeter harsh taste and a wonderful pink colour. Here I have gone for the classical gooseberry-elderflower combination because you just can't beat it. The mousse is very, very light, just right for summer.

The elderflower could be replaced with meadowsweet and the gooseberries with rhubarb.

Serves 8

for *the elderflower mousse*
2¹/₂ *gelatine leaves*
50ml milk
4 good heads of elderflower, finely chopped
5 eggs, separated
20g plain flour
150g caster sugar
50ml water
150ml lemon juice
75ml double cream, lightly whipped
icing sugar for dusting

for *the roasted red gooseberries*
150g golden caster sugar
1 head of elderflowers, chopped
grated zest of 1 orange
500g red gooseberries, trimmed

elderflower mousse
Soften the gelatine in cold water for about 5 minutes, until soft and pliable. Put the milk in a small saucepan with the elderflowers and bring to boiling point. Meanwhile, whisk the egg yolks and flour together. Pour the milk on to them, whisking constantly, then return the mixture to the pan and cook, stirring, over a medium heat until thick. Remove from the heat. Squeeze all the water out of the gelatine and add the gelatine to the pan, beating well. Pass the mixture through a fine sieve into a bowl and set aside.

Place 100g of the caster sugar in a small saucepan with the water and heat gently, stirring to dissolve the sugar. Raise the heat, bring to the boil and cook without stirring until it reaches soft-ball stage (120°C on a sugar thermometer). Meanwhile, in a freestanding electric mixer, whisk the egg whites with the lemon juice and the remaining sugar until they form soft peaks. When the syrup reaches the correct temperature, pour it on to the egg whites in a thin stream with the machine running. Whisk until cold.

Carefully fold the whipped cream into the egg yolk mixture, followed by the egg whites. Grease 8 rings, 7cm in diameter and 4cm high, and wrap the bases in cling film. Fill with the mousse, then cover and leave in the fridge for 3–4 hours, until set.

roasted red gooseberries
Place the sugar, elderflowers and orange zest in a food processor and pulse until broken down to a coarse powder. Remove and sprinkle over the gooseberries. Mix well and place in a single layer on a buttered baking tray, being sure to include all the sugar.

Place in an oven preheated to 250°C/Gas Mark 10 and cook for 7–15 minutes, until the gooseberries are just tender but still hold their shape. The time will vary according to the size and ripeness of the gooseberries. Remove from the oven and leave to cool.

serving
Carefully remove the elderflower mousses from the ring moulds and dust the tops heavily with icing sugar. Quickly blowtorch the surface to create an even, golden-brown crust. Place on serving plates and add the gooseberries, drizzling them with their juices.

meadowsweet cream with meadowsweet and greengage sorbet and breton butter biscuits

Meadowsweet can be seen all over the countryside in the summer. It is so prolific that it is worth gathering a lot and drying it. The creamy white flowers, with their intoxicatingly sweet fragrance, make a natural addition to desserts. Here I have paired them with greengages, my favourite member of the plum family – I just love their tartness.

The Breton butter biscuits are traditionally made with salted butter from Brittany but you could use good local salted butter if you can find it.

Serves 8

for the meadowsweet and greengage sorbet
750g greengages, halved and stoned
10g fresh meadowsweet flowers, roughly
    chopped
130g caster sugar
1¹/₂ gelatine leaves
200ml water
juice of ¹/₂ lemon

for the meadowsweet cream
juice of 1 lemon
25g fresh meadowsweet flowers
500ml double cream
100ml milk
75g caster sugar
1³/₄ gelatine leaves

for the breton butter biscuits
300g salted butter
175g icing sugar
3 egg yolks
300g plain flour
a dash of orange flower water

for the greengages
16 ripe greengages, halved and stoned
    (keep 4 of the stones)
300ml water
200g caster sugar
juice of 1 lemon
5g fresh meadowsweet flowers

meadowsweet and greengage sorbet
Place the greengages in a bowl with the meadowsweet and sugar and leave in the fridge overnight to allow the flavours to develop.

The next day, soak the gelatine in cold water for about 5 minutes, until soft and pliable. Put the water and lemon juice in a saucepan and bring to the boil. Add the greengages and their juices, bring back to the boil and immediately place in a liquidiser. Blend until smooth, then pass through a fine sieve. Squeeze all the water out of the gelatine and whisk the gelatine into the greengage purée until dissolved. Leave to cool. Place in an ice-cream machine and freeze according to the manufacturer's instructions. Transfer to the fridge to soften slightly about 10 minutes before serving.

meadowsweet cream
Put the lemon juice and meadowsweet in a saucepan, bring to the boil, then add the double cream, milk and sugar and bring back to the boil. Pull to one side and leave to infuse for about 2 hours.

Soak the gelatine in cold water for about 5 minutes, until soft and pliable, then remove and squeeze out all the water. Bring the meadowsweet mixture back to the boil and then pass through a fine sieve. Whisk in the softened gelatine until dissolved. Use cling film to line 8 tart tins, 10cm in diameter and 2.5cm deep, then pour in the mixture, filling them half way. Place in the fridge to set.

breton butter biscuits
Place the butter and icing sugar in a mixing bowl and cream together until white. Add 1 egg yolk, sift in a third of the flour and mix well. Repeat twice until all the egg yolks and flour are used up. Beat in the orange flower water. Grease 8 tart tins, 10cm in diameter and 2.5cm deep, and pipe the mixture into them; it should be quite soft. Place in an oven preheated to 180°C/Gas Mark 4 and bake for 15–20 minutes, until golden brown; the biscuits will crisp up on cooling. Remove them from the tins and place on a wire rack to cool. Store in an airtight container.

greengages
Crack the 4 reserved greengage stones with a rolling pin and place in a large saucepan with the water, sugar, lemon juice and meadowsweet. Bring to the boil, stirring to dissolve the sugar, and simmer for 2–3 minutes. Remove from the heat and add the greengages. Let them cook in the residual heat for 2–3 minutes. When they are tender but not mushy, lift them out with a slotted spoon and cool down quickly. When the syrup is cool, return the greengages to it.

serving
Put a Breton butter biscuit on each serving plate. Remove the meadowsweet creams from the fridge, turn them out of the tins and place on top of the biscuits. Arrange the greengages on the creams and finally place a scoop of sorbet on top.

gorse flower panna cotta with gorse and coconut sorbet

There are a lot of gorse bushes growing near us in Cheltenham and if we brush past them in late spring, when the sun is on them, they smell of a certain suntan lotion with a very strong hint of coconut. The flowers are available nearly all year round but they are at their best at this time of year. We pick them at this stage and dry them for a couple of days to intensify the scent and flavour. To dry them at home, scatter them over a tray and leave in a warm place, such as an airing cupboard, for a day or so.

Blackcurrant leaves could be used for a different flavour if you don't like gorse.

Serves 6–8

for the gorse and coconut sorbet
250ml coconut milk
25g coconut powder
50g dried gorse flowers
150g caster sugar
40ml liquid glucose
75ml double cream
200ml water
$^1/_2$ gelatine leaf
25ml Malibu

for the gorse flower panna cotta
700ml double cream
100ml milk
100g dried gorse flowers
110g caster sugar
3 gelatine leaves

for the coconut tuiles
30ml coconut milk
20g unsalted butter, melted
20g rice flour
50g icing sugar

to serve
50g Cardamom Yoghurt (see page 18)

gorse and coconut sorbet
Put all the ingredients except the gelatine and Malibu in a saucepan, whisk well, then bring to the boil, whisking from time to time. Meanwhile, soak the gelatine in cold water for about 5 minutes, until soft and pliable. Remove and squeeze out all the water.

When the coconut mixture comes to the boil, remove from the heat and add the gelatine, stirring until dissolved. Pass through a fine sieve and leave to cool, then add the Malibu. Place in an ice-cream machine and freeze according to the manufacturer's instructions. Transfer to the fridge to soften slightly about 10 minutes before serving.

gorse flower panna cotta
Put the cream, milk, gorse flowers and sugar in a heavy-based saucepan and bring gently to the boil. Pull to the side of the stove and leave to infuse for 40 minutes, to extract as much of the gorse flavour as you can.

Soak the gelatine in cold water for about 5 minutes, until soft and pliable, then remove and squeeze out all the water. Bring the gorse mixture back to the boil, remove from the heat again and whisk in the gelatine, making sure it has dissolved. Strain the mixture through a fine sieve, pressing on the gorse to extract as much juice as you can. Leave to cool, then pour into lightly oiled dariole moulds, about 130ml in capacity, cover and leave in the fridge to set.

coconut tuiles
Put all the ingredients in a bowl and beat well. Place in the fridge for 2 hours to firm up a little. Brush the mixture on to a lined baking sheet in rectangles measuring 2 x 5cm. Bake in an oven preheated to 180°C/Gas Mark 4 for approximately 5 minutes, until golden brown. Remove from the oven and leave to cool, then lift off the baking sheet with a palette knife. Store in a sealed container.

serving
Dip the panna cotta moulds in hot water for 2–3 seconds, gently pull the mixture away from the side of the moulds and quickly turn out on to serving plates. Serve with a scoop of sorbet, a slash of cardamom yoghurt and a coconut tuile.

sorrel ice cream with wood sorrel and compote of brambles

The idea for this came to me when I was making a dessert with lemon verbena and I wondered what it would be like using sorrel instead. They both have a lemony flavour, so it seemed only logical. Then we encountered a problem, since, as everyone who has used sorrel will know, it turns brown when exposed to heat. After several experiments, we found that adding ascorbic acid stopped the oxidisation, and as long as it was done quickly the colour was retained. The flavour is so refreshing. Here we have served it with brambles (wild blackberries).

Serves 6

for the sorrel ice cream
300ml milk
200ml double cream
6 egg yolks
60g caster sugar
10g milk powder
10ml liquid glucose
7g ascorbic acid
75g sorrel

for the bramble compote
750g brambles
100g caster sugar
1 gelatine leaf
juice of 1 lemon

to serve
25g wood sorrel

sorrel ice cream
Gently bring the milk and cream to the boil in a heavy-based saucepan. Meanwhile, whisk the egg yolks with the sugar, milk powder and glucose until pale and creamy. Pour half the milk mixture on to the eggs, whisking to combine, then pour this back into the saucepan. Cook over a gentle heat, stirring constantly with a wooden spoon, until the mixture thickens enough to coat the back of the spoon (it should register about 84°C on a thermometer). Remove from the heat, add the ascorbic acid and sorrel, then transfer to a liquidiser and purée until the sorrel has completely disappeared and you are left with a vivid green liquid. Strain immediately through a fine sieve into a large bowl. Freeze in an ice-cream machine according to the manufacturer's instructions. Transfer to the fridge to soften slightly about 10 minutes before serving.

bramble compote
Lightly cook the brambles with the sugar until the juices just start to run; do not cook them for too long or they will become mushy. Meanwhile, soak the gelatine in cold water for about 5 minutes, until soft and pliable.

Drain the berries gently, being careful not to let them break up. Place the juice and 50g of the brambles in a liquidiser and blend until smooth. Add the lemon juice and strain through a fine sieve, pushing through as much of the fruit as you can. Squeeze the water out of the gelatine, add the gelatine to the hot purée and stir until dissolved. Leave to cool, then add the remaining brambles.

serving
Arrange the brambles on serving plates and drizzle with a little of the juice. Place a large scoop of sorrel ice cream on the plate and decorate with the wood sorrel.

camomile cream with soft meringue, brambles and sugared verbena

I am sure that when you are walking anywhere you will pass lots of camomile. The little flowers resemble daisies, and if you pick one and squeeze the centre it should smell faintly of pineapple or fresh green apple – something that is lost when it is dried. Here the camomile cream is served in the middle of a soft meringue, which is so moreish you will just want a bigger piece.

There are many alternative flavourings for the cream: mandarin zest, chopped prunes or chocolate, for a start. The compote is flavoured with verbena leaves, with their wonderful lemon scent.

Serves 8

for the camomile cream
450ml milk
30g fresh chamomile flowers
2 eggs
1 egg yolk
75g caster sugar
50g cornflour
100g unsalted butter, diced
1¹/₂ gelatine leaves
30ml lemon juice
125ml double cream, whipped

for the soft meringue
300g egg whites (8–9 whites)
5ml lemon juice
400g caster sugar
5g cornflour

for the sugared verbena
2 egg whites
24 lemon verbena leaves
50g caster sugar

for the bramble compote
500g brambles
80g caster sugar
5 lemon verbena leaves
1¹/₂ gelatine leaves
juice of 1 lemon

camomile cream
Put the milk and camomile in a heavy-based saucepan and bring to the boil. Meanwhile, whisk the eggs, egg yolk, sugar and cornflour together. Gradually pour in the milk, whisking to combine, then return the mixture to the pan and cook over a medium heat for 4–5 minutes, stirring constantly, until thick. Remove from the heat, place to one side to cool a little, then stir in the butter bit by bit until it has melted. Soak the gelatine in cold water for 5 minutes until soft and pliable. Squeeze out all the water, add the gelatine to the camomile mixture and stir until dissolved. Stir in the lemon juice.

Pass the mixture through a fine sieve into a bowl. Cover the surface with cling film and leave to cool. Fold in the double cream, then cover and store in the fridge until needed.

soft meringue
Using an electric mixer, whisk the egg whites on high speed until frothy. Add the lemon juice and a third of the sugar and whisk until the whites form soft peaks. Whisk in another third of the sugar, then rain in the remaining third with the cornflour and continue whisking until stiff peaks form.

Use baking parchment to line a 54 x 32cm baking tray (or two 25 x 36cm trays) and spread the meringue over it. Place in an oven preheated to 160°C/Gas Mark 3 and bake for 20 minutes; the top should be cracked and the meringue still a little moist. Remove from the oven and leave to cool.

Turn the meringue out of the tin on to a board so the lining paper is now on top. Peel off the paper and spread the chamomile cream evenly over the meringue in a layer about 1cm thick. Roll it up as if it were a swiss roll, then roll it tightly in cling film. Leave in the fridge for 2–4 hours to set the shape.

sugared verbena
Whisk the egg whites until foamy, just to break them down a little. Dip the verbena leaves in the egg white, remove the excess and then dip in the caster sugar. Turn the leaves over a few times until thoroughly coated. Shake off excess sugar and place the leaves on a baking sheet lined with baking parchment, making sure they don't touch each other. Place in an oven preheated to 100°C (or a very low gas oven) and leave for 1–1¹/₂ hours, until the leaves have become dry and crisp. Remove from the oven, allow to cool, then store in an airtight container.

bramble compote
Lightly cook the brambles with the sugar and lemon verbena until the juices just start to run; do not cook them for too long or they will become mushy. Meanwhile, soak the gelatine in cold water for about 5 minutes, until soft and pliable. Drain the berries gently, being careful not to let them break up. Place the juice and 50g of the brambles in a liquidiser and blend until smooth. Add the lemon juice and strain through a fine sieve, pushing through as much of the fruit as you can. Squeeze the water out of the gelatine, add the gelatine to the hot purée and stir until dissolved. Leave to cool, then add the remaining brambles.

serving
Remove the meringue from the fridge, cut it into slices through the cling film and take off the cling film as you place the meringue on serving plates. Spoon some compote next to the meringue and garnish with the sugared leaves.

chestnut flan with bramley purée and lait de poule

This is a lovely little autumn pre-dessert, with the apple purée adding a touch of acidity to balance the chestnuts. We are in the happy position of having chestnut trees growing near where we live, and when we take our dogs for a walk we make great use of nature's bounty.

In Gascony they sometimes substitute white beans for chestnuts in their recipes. Although beans don't taste the same, they do have a similar texture. Do try it if you are feeling adventurous; it works quite well here.

The lait de poule is something I have had in France and is basically a frothy custard.

Serves 12 as a pre-dessert, 6 as a dessert

for the chestnut flan
100g chestnut purée
450ml double cream
1 egg
2 egg yolks
50g caster sugar
10ml rum

for the Bramley purée
420g Bramley apples, peeled and cored
juice of 1/2 lemon
10g unsalted butter
25g caster sugar

for the lait de poule
400ml milk
100ml double cream
2 eggs
4 egg yolks
50g caster sugar
30ml rum

chestnut flan
Place the chestnut purée in a saucepan, whisk in the double cream and bring to the boil, stirring all the time. Remove from the heat.

Whisk the egg, egg yolks and caster sugar together, then pour on the chestnut mixture, stirring to combine. Return to the pan and warm through on a low heat for 2 minutes, stirring constantly, but do not cook it. Remove from the heat and stir in the rum. Pass through a fine sieve into a measuring jug. Pour the mixture into heatproof glasses, filling them a third full, and place in a roasting tin. Pour enough hot water into the tin to come half way up the side of the glasses, then place in an oven preheated to 120°C/Gas Mark 1/2. Cook for 20 minutes or until just set. Remove from the oven, leave to cool and then place in the fridge to chill.

bramley purée
Slice the apples finely and mix them with the lemon juice. Heat the butter in a saucepan, add the sugar and apples and cook over a medium heat, stirring occasionally, until the apples have broken down. Place in a liquidiser or food processor and blend until smooth. Check to see if you need to add a little more sugar or lemon juice. Leave to cool, then chill until needed.

lait de poule
Bring the milk and cream to the boil in a saucepan. Meanwhile, whisk the eggs, egg yolks and sugar together in a bowl. Pour on the hot milk, whisking to combine, then return the mixture to the saucepan, and cook, stirring constantly with a wooden spoon, until it has thickened slightly; it should be the consistency of single cream. Pass through a fine sieve into a bowl and leave to cool. Add the rum and then chill.

serving
Remove the chestnut flans from the fridge and leave at room temperature for 10 minutes. Cover each one with a layer of Bramley purée. Froth the lait de poule with a hand blender or in a liquidiser and carefully pour it over the purée, nearly filling the glasses. Serve immediately.

chestnut cake with chestnut sorbet

This is just one of the desserts we can make after gathering chestnuts on our walks with the dogs. The cake has a lovely nutty taste and includes just a little chocolate, which goes so well with chestnuts. A little thyme or lavender would also be good. It can be made without the cornflour if you wish to make a totally flourless cake. The sorbet goes well with apple, pear and quince.

To peel chestnuts, heavily score each one with a sharp knife, digging into the skin a little, then place them in a pan of boiling water for about 3 minutes. Leave in the water while peeling a few at a time, being sure to remove the thin brown inner skin as well as the shell.

Serves 8

for the chestnut sorbet
300g peeled chestnuts
100g caster sugar
800ml water
250ml milk
100ml liquid glucose
50ml rum

for the chestnut cake
300ml milk
500g peeled chestnuts
4 eggs
100g bitter chocolate (64 per cent cocoa solids), chopped
100g unsalted butter
100g caster sugar
10g cornflour
70g ground almonds
grated zest of 1 lemon
icing sugar for dusting

for the poached chestnuts
200g caster sugar
125ml water
1/2 vanilla pod, split open lengthwise
a strip of orange zest
8 large, peeled chestnuts

chestnut sorbet
Place the chestnuts, sugar and water in a saucepan and bring to the boil, stirring to dissolve the sugar. Simmer for about 30 minutes, until the chestnuts are soft. Add the milk and glucose, bring back to the boil, then remove from the heat. Blend the mixture to a smooth purée in a liquidiser, push through a fine sieve and leave to cool. Stir in the rum. Freeze the mixture in an ice-cream machine according to the manufacturer's instructions. Transfer to the fridge to soften slightly about 10 minutes before serving.

chestnut cake
Put the milk and chestnuts in a saucepan and bring to the boil. Reduce the heat to a simmer and cook for about 30 minutes, until soft. Blend to a smooth purée in a liquidiser, then set aside.

Place the eggs in their shells in a bowl of warm water for 10 minutes before using. Put the chopped chocolate in a bowl and melt over a pan of simmering water or in a microwave (see page 23). Add the butter and stir until melted, then set aside. Crack the eggs into a mixing bowl, add the caster sugar and whisk until thick and creamy. Put this to one side too.

Add the cornflour to the ground almonds. Fold the chocolate mixture into the chestnut purée and then fold in the whisked eggs, incorporating them gently but evenly. Finally fold in the ground almonds, cornflour and lemon zest. Butter and line a loose-bottomed 20cm cake tin, 3cm deep. Transfer the mixture to it and bake in an oven preheated to 180°C/Gas Mark 4 for 40–50 minutes, until a knife inserted in the centre comes out clean. Remove from the oven and allow to cool for 10 minutes before removing from the tin.

poached chestnuts
Place all the ingredients except the chestnuts in a pan and bring to the boil. Simmer for 2–3 minutes, then add the chestnuts and simmer for 15 minutes, until tender. Remove from the heat and leave to cool. The chestnuts can be kept, covered in the syrup, in the fridge for 1–2 weeks.

serving
Turn the cake out of the tin and cut it into 8 slices. Dust with icing sugar and serve with a scoop of chestnut sorbet and a poached chestnut.

craquant of rowanberry cream with cobnut purée

Rowan trees are fairly prolific in Britain, so it makes great sense to use their wonderful fruit. The orangey-red berries are ripest when their colour is at its deepest, and this is when you should pick them. The sharp flavour has a hint of marmalade when cooked with sugar. They make a perfect partner to crab apples, which coincidentally are around at the same time.

Cobnuts, also called filberts or hazelnuts, are a common hedgerow tree, so it is well worth scouring your area for any. They are in season from August to early November. There is something different about the wild ones. I think they taste a little sweeter, but maybe that is just because they are free!

Serves 6

for the rowanberry cream
400g rowanberries
150g caster sugar
400ml milk
2 eggs
2 egg yolks
50g cornflour
100g unsalted butter
2 gelatine leaves
125ml double cream, lightly whipped

for the cobnut craquant
200ml liquid glucose
200g caster sugar
50ml water
100g cobnuts, lightly toasted and then
    skinned

for the cobnut purée
150g cobnuts, lightly toasted and then
    skinned
200ml milk
25g caster sugar

to serve
50g cobnuts, finely sliced

rowanberry cream
Place the rowanberries and half the sugar in a saucepan and bring to the boil, stirring to dissolve the sugar. Simmer for 5 minutes, then place in a liquidiser and blend to a smooth purée. Pass through a fine sieve, return the mixture to the pan and bring to the boil. Simmer until the purée has thickened and reduced in volume by half.

Bring the milk to the boil in a heavy-based saucepan. Meanwhile, whisk the eggs, egg yolks, cornflour and remaining sugar together in a bowl. Add the hot milk, whisking to combine, then return the mixture to the saucepan. Cook over a medium heat for 4–5 minutes, stirring constantly, until thick. Remove from the heat, place to one side to cool a little, then stir in the butter bit by bit until completely melted. Soak the gelatine in cold water for about 5 minutes, until soft and pliable, then squeeze out all the water and add the gelatine to the mixture. Stir until dissolved, then add the rowan purée. Pass the mixture through a fine sieve into a bowl, lay a little cling film directly on top and leave to cool. Fold in the double cream, then cover and store in the fridge.

cobnut craquant
Put the glucose, caster sugar and water in a heavy-based saucepan and heat gently, stirring to dissolve the sugar. Bring to the boil and cook without stirring until it has turned into a golden, amber caramel. Add the cobnuts and swirl around to coat them in the caramel, then pour immediately on to an oiled baking tray. Set to one side until cold and very crisp. Break up the caramel, place in a food processor and pulse to a coarse powder. Store in an airtight container.

Shortly before serving, sprinkle the craquant powder over a lined baking tray in an even layer to form a large rectangle. Place in an oven preheated to 200°C/Gas Mark 6 until it has melted and formed a single sheet of caramel; it will take only a minute or two, so be very vigilant. Remove from the oven, let it cool and, just before it sets, cut it into strips measuring 12 x 4cm. You will need 18 but it's worth making 24, just in case, as they are very brittle. Keep the trimmings because they can be ground down and used again. Store the strips in an airtight container with baking parchment between the layers.

cobnut purée
Place the cobnuts, milk and sugar in a saucepan and bring to the boil, stirring to dissolve the sugar. Simmer for 20 minutes, then remove from the heat. Place in a liquidiser and blend until smooth. It should be the consistency of thick custard – if it is too thick, add a little more milk. Leave to cool, then cover and store in the fridge.

serving
Beat the rowanberry cream well and place in a piping bag. Lay out 12 craquant strips and pipe the rowanberry cream on top to cover. Place 6 of them on top of the other 6, then top with the remaining unpiped craquants. Place 2 streaks of cobnut purée on each serving plate, carefully lift the craquants on to the plates and scatter with the sliced cobnuts.

elderberry vacherin with elderberry curd

Originally a vacherin consisted of ice cream served in a meringue nest that resembled the cheese of the same name. Then a sorbet was added and the shape changed, so this is our rather modern interpretation of the vacherin. I am a big fan of elderberries. With their deep purple colour and their lovely tartness, they make a great foil for the meringue.

If you can't get elderberries, try brambles instead. If you wish to vary the ice cream, an orange one would work, as would lemon verbena or lemon balm.

Serves 8

for the vanilla ice cream
3 vanilla pods
625ml milk
50g milk powder
175ml double cream
8 egg yolks
125g caster sugar
25ml liquid glucose

for the elderberry sorbet
1 gelatine leaf
500g elderberries
200ml water
125g caster sugar
juice of 1/2 lemon

for the elderberry curd
250g elderberries
75g caster sugar
2 eggs
2 egg yolks
3g cornflour
75g unsalted butter, diced

for the meringue
100g egg whites (3–4 whites)
a pinch of salt
juice of 1/2 lemon
200g caster sugar

to serve
200g blueberries

vanilla ice cream
Slit the vanilla pods lengthwise in half, scrape out the seeds and place in a heavy-based saucepan with the milk, milk powder and cream. Bring gently to just below the boil, then remove from the heat and leave to infuse for 2 hours or even overnight. Gently bring to the boil again. Meanwhile, whisk the egg yolks with the sugar and glucose until pale and creamy. Pour half the milk mixture on to the eggs, whisking to combine, then pour this back into the saucepan. Cook over a gentle heat, stirring constantly with a wooden spoon, until the mixture thickens enough to coat the back of the spoon (it should register about 84°C on a thermometer). Strain immediately through a fine sieve into a large bowl to help stop the cooking and leave to cool. Freeze in an ice-cream machine according to the manufacturer's instructions. Transfer to the fridge to soften slightly about 10 minutes before serving.

elderberry sorbet
Soak the gelatine in cold water for about 5 minutes, until soft and pliable. Place the elderberries, water and caster sugar in a saucepan and bring to the boil, stirring to dissolve the sugar. Simmer for 5 minutes, then transfer to a liquidiser and blend to a smooth purée. Pass through a fine sieve. Squeeze all the water out of the gelatine, add it to the purée and stir until dissolved. Stir in the lemon juice, leave to cool, then churn in an ice-cream machine according to the manufacturer's instructions. Place in 2 terrine moulds and keep in the freezer until needed.

elderberry curd
Place the elderberries in a saucepan with the sugar and bring to the boil, stirring to dissolve the sugar. Simmer for 2 minutes, then transfer to a liquidiser and blend until smooth. Whisk the eggs, egg yolks and cornflour together. Pour the elderberry purée on to the egg yolks, whisking to combine, then return to the pan. Cook over a medium heat until the mixture has thickened; do not let it boil or the eggs will scramble. Remove from the heat, cool slightly, then add the butter bit by bit, letting each piece melt before adding the next. Pass through a fine sieve and leave to cool. Store in an airtight container in the fridge until needed.

meringue
Using an electric mixer, whisk the egg whites, salt and lemon juice on high speed until the whites start to froth. Add half the sugar and whisk until the whites form soft peaks. With the machine still on full, rain in the remaining sugar and whisk until the meringue is shiny and stiff.

Line a baking sheet with baking parchment, then place about a tablespoon of meringue on the parchment and spread it with your spoon in a quick movement so it looks like a little wing. Repeat until you have used all the meringue; you will need 24 but as they are very brittle, make 30 just in case. Place in an oven preheated to 120°C/Gas Mark 1/2 and cook for about an hour. Remove from the oven and allow to cool for a few minutes; the meringues should be crisp and lift from the paper very easily. If they are slightly soggy, place back in the oven for a little longer. Leave to cool, then store in an airtight container.

serving
Place a swipe of the elderberry curd on each serving plate, then a slice of the elderberry sorbet. Scatter with the blueberries. Pipe a spiral of ice cream on to 2 of the meringue 'wings', then stack them on top of each other and place a third ' wing' on top. Pipe a small rosette of ice cream on top of the sorbet to anchor the meringue and place the meringue sandwich on top at an angle.

acorn tiramisu

Tiramisu is a dessert that everyone knows and loves. It has gained a reputation for being a good dish for entertaining, since it is relatively easy to make, and I have certainly had it at a few dinner parties. The secret is to make it light and moist. Here, instead of using espresso coffee for soaking the sponge fingers, I have made a strong acorn 'coffee'. The acorns have a complex flavour of spiced chocolate, caramel and almonds. Be careful not to over cook them or they will be too bitter. If you can't get acorns, you could substitute chicory root.

Serves 12

for the acorn 'coffee'
150g acorns
50g caster sugar
400ml water

for the sponge fingers
6 eggs
200g caster sugar, plus 30g for sprinkling
130g plain flour
20g cornflour
1/4 teaspoon baking powder
1 teaspoon vanilla extract

for the chestnut tuiles
140g chestnut flour
200g icing sugar
120g unsalted butter, melted
25g chestnut honey
3 egg whites

for the tiramisu
2 eggs, separated
55g caster sugar
450g mascarpone cheese
150ml double cream, whipped to stiff peaks
30g icing sugar
30ml rum
30ml Tia Maria
cocoa powder for dusting
125g bitter chocolate (71 per cent cocoa solids), melted
icing sugar for dusting

acorn 'coffee'
Shell the acorns, put them on a baking tray and place in an oven preheated to 150°C/ Gas Mark 2. Roast for 15–20 minutes, until they are a deep brown colour, being careful not to let them burn or they will taste very bitter. Leave to cool, then grind to a coarse powder in a spice grinder or coffee grinder.

Put the sugar, water and ground acorns in a saucepan and bring gently to the boil, stirring to dissolve the sugar. Pull to the side of the stove and leave to infuse for 40 minutes, to extract as much of the acorns' flavour as possible. Pass through a fine sieve and leave to cool.

sponge fingers
Place the eggs in their shells in a bowl of warm water for 5 minutes before using. Remove the eggs from the water and separate them, placing the yolks in a mixing bowl with half the sugar. Whisk until very thick and white, then set aside. In a separate bowl, whisk the whites until they form medium peaks. Slowly rain in the rest of the sugar and continue to whisk until they form stiff peaks. Carefully fold the whites into the yolks. Sift the flour, cornflour and baking powder together, then sift them again into the egg mix, lightly folding in all the time. Finally add the vanilla. Try not to over work the mixture or you will knock out the air.

Place the mixture in a piping bag fitted with a 1.5cm nozzle and pipe into 6–8cm cylinders on baking sheets lined with baking parchment; there should be about 40 altogether. Sprinkle with the 30g caster sugar. Place in an oven preheated to 180°C/ Gas Mark 4 and bake for 15–20 minutes, until light brown. Remove from the oven, leave to cool, then store in an airtight container.

chestnut tuiles
Place the chestnut flour and icing sugar in a bowl, add the butter and honey and beat until smooth. Beat in the egg whites, then chill for 2 hours. Remove the mixture from the fridge and spread it out in thin strips, about 1 x 5cm, on a baking sheet lined with baking parchment. Place in an oven preheated to 180°C/Gas Mark 4 and bake for 5–8 minutes, until golden. Remove from the oven, cool slightly, then lift the tuiles off the tray. Gently place in an airtight container.

tiramisu
Whisk the egg yolks with the caster sugar until very thick and pale. In a separate bowl, beat the mascarpone to make it smooth. Fold in the whipped cream, then gently fold in the egg yolk mixture. Whisk the egg whites until they form soft peaks, then add the icing sugar and whisk to stiff peaks. Gently fold the whites into the mascarpone mixture.

Take 250ml of the acorn 'coffee' and stir in the rum and Tia Maria. Line a 36 x 11.5 x 4cm metal cooking frame with cling film and place on a baking tray. Dip the sponge fingers in the acorn 'coffee' for 10–20 seconds, then cover the bottom of the lined mould with a layer of sponge fingers placed side by side. Spread a third of the mascarpone mix on top. Dust with a little cocoa powder, then drizzle with half the melted chocolate. Repeat the process with the sponge, then the mascarpone etc, then repeat one final time, leaving out the chocolate and the cocoa powder on the last layer. Place in the fridge until needed.

serving
Dust the tiramisu with a little cocoa powder and cut it into slices. Place on plates and arrange the tuiles on top, then dust with a little icing sugar. I like to serve this with a good strong espresso.

carrageen moss blancmange with lemongrass ice cream

I envy those lucky enough to live near the coast and have access to fresh carrageen – they have a wonderful wild product for free. Carrageen moss is not really a moss at all. It is, of course, a seaweed, and can be used fresh, dried or even powdered. This recipe uses the dried version, which is readily available from herbalists or healthfood shops. It is a great natural setting agent with a neutral taste. Here I have flavoured the blancmange with lemon, orange and vanilla, although it is really down to you to inject flavours that you like into the dish. The lemongrass ice cream complements it rather well, as do the raspberries.

If you want to serve the blancmange in glasses, 5g of carrageen will be enough for a light set.

Serves 8

for the lemongrass ice cream
juice and grated zest of 2 lemons
350ml double cream
750ml milk
3 lemongrass stalks, chopped
8 egg yolks
20ml liquid glucose
200g caster sugar

for the carrageen moss blancmange
7.5g carrageen moss
700ml milk
200ml double cream
2 strips of orange zest
2 strips of lemon zest
1 vanilla pod, slit open lengthwise
1 egg
75g caster sugar
a few drops of orange flower water, to taste

for the raspberries
400g raspberries
50g caster sugar
juice of 1/4 lemon

lemongrass ice cream
Put the lemon juice and zest in a heavy-based saucepan, bring to the boil and simmer for 1 minute. Add the cream, milk and chopped lemongrass and bring gently to just below the boil. Remove from the heat and leave to infuse for 2 hours or even overnight.

Gently bring to the boil again. Meanwhile, whisk the egg yolks with the glucose and sugar until pale and creamy. Pour half the milk mixture on to the egg yolks, whisking to combine, then pour this back into the saucepan. Cook over a gentle heat, stirring constantly with a wooden spoon, until the mixture thickens enough to coat the back of the spoon (it should register about 84°C on a thermometer). Immediately strain through a fine sieve into a large bowl to help stop the cooking, pushing down to extract as much of the lemongrass flavour as possible. Leave to cool, then freeze in an ice-cream machine according to the manufacturer's instructions. Transfer to the fridge to soften slightly about 10 minutes before serving.

carrageen moss blancmange
Place the moss in a little warm water, not too hot, for about 5 minutes to plump up and soften a little. Put the milk, cream, split vanilla pod and orange and lemon zest in a saucepan and bring to the boil. Squeeze out the water from the moss and add the moss to the saucepan. Stir well and simmer for 10 minutes, stirring occasionally. Remove from the heat.

Whisk the egg with the sugar until frothy and then gradually pour on the moss milk, whisking constantly. Pass through a fine sieve into a measuring jug and then pour into 8 lightly oiled dariole moulds, 120–130ml in capacity. Leave to cool. You can either serve them warm after about 40 minutes, when they will be set enough to turn out, or cover and place in the fridge for 2–3 hours until thoroughly chilled.

raspberries
Place 100g of the raspberries in a liquidiser with the sugar and lemon juice and blend until smooth. Pass through a fine sieve. Place the remaining raspberries in a bowl, add the purée and mix lightly to coat.

serving
Dip the moulds in hot water for 2–3 seconds, then gently pull the blancmange away from the sides of the moulds and quickly turn out on to serving dishes. Place some of the raspberries on the plate and a scoop of ice cream to the side.

crab apple and walnut crumble with crumble ice cream

Crab apples are one of my favourite wild foods. They are very high in pectin, so if you want to make a preserve of apple, or bramble and apple, jelly, these are the ones to use.

This is my take on an apple crumble. The walnut crumble is made first and then baked till extra crisp. The crab apple comes in two forms – a purée and a compote.

Serves 8

for the walnut crumble mix
75g brioche
75g walnuts
75g unsalted butter, melted
30g cornflour
2 egg whites, lightly whisked
75g icing sugar

for the crab apple purée
700g crab apples, peeled and cored
juice of 1/2 lemon
25g unsalted butter
100g caster sugar

for the crumble ice cream
500ml milk
250ml double cream
125g crab apple purée (see below)
150g walnut crumble mix (see below)
6 egg yolks
125g caster sugar

for the apple tuiles
150ml apple juice, boiled until reduced to 30ml
25g unsalted butter, melted
25g rice flour
50g icing sugar

for the crab apple compote
125g caster sugar
150ml water
a strip of orange zest
seeds from 1/2 vanilla pod
juice of 1/2 lemon
350g larger crab apples, cored and peeled

to serve
10g apple blossoms

walnut crumble mix
Cut the brioche into 3mm dice and break up the walnuts to the same size. Place in a bowl and mix with the melted butter. Allow the bread to soak up the butter for 5 minutes, then add the cornflour and egg whites. Mix well and spread out evenly over a baking sheet lined with baking parchment. Place in an oven preheated to 160°C/Gas Mark 3 and bake for about 20 minutes, until pale golden brown. Remove from the oven and leave to cool.

Break the mixture into small pieces and place in a bowl. Add the icing sugar and mix thoroughly, coating all the bits evenly. Scatter back on to the lined baking sheet and return it to the oven for 5–8 minutes to crisp up more and get a deeper golden colour. Leave to cool, then break up evenly and store in an airtight container until needed.

crab apple purée
Chop the apples roughly and mix them with the lemon juice. Heat the butter in a saucepan, add the sugar and apples and cook over a medium heat, stirring occasionally, until the apples have broken down. Place in a liquidiser or food processor and blend until smooth. Return to the pan and cook, stirring regularly, until it reduces to a stiff purée. Check to see if you need to add a little more sugar or lemon juice, then leave to cool. Chill until needed.

crumble ice cream
In a heavy-based saucepan, gently bring the milk and cream to just below the boil, then remove from the heat. Whisk in the crab apple purée and stir in the crumble mix. Leave to infuse for 2 hours or even overnight.

Pass the mixture through a fine sieve into a saucepan and bring gently to the boil. Meanwhile, whisk the egg yolks with the sugar until pale and creamy. Pour half the milk mixture on to the egg yolks, whisking to combine, then pour this back into the saucepan. Cook over a gentle heat, stirring constantly with a wooden spoon, until the mixture thickens enough to coat the back of the spoon (it should register about 84°C on a thermometer). Strain immediately through a fine sieve into a large bowl to help stop the cooking. Leave to cool, then freeze in an ice-cream machine according to the manufacturer's instructions. Transfer to the fridge to soften slightly about 10 minutes before serving.

apple tuiles
Put all the ingredients in a bowl and beat well. Place in the fridge for 2 hours to firm up a little. Brush the mixture on to a lined baking sheet in rectangles measuring 2 x 6cm. Place in an oven preheated to 180°C/Gas Mark 4 and bake for about 5 minutes, until golden brown. Remove from the oven and leave to cool, then lift off the baking sheet with a palette knife. Store in a sealed container.

(continued on page 135)

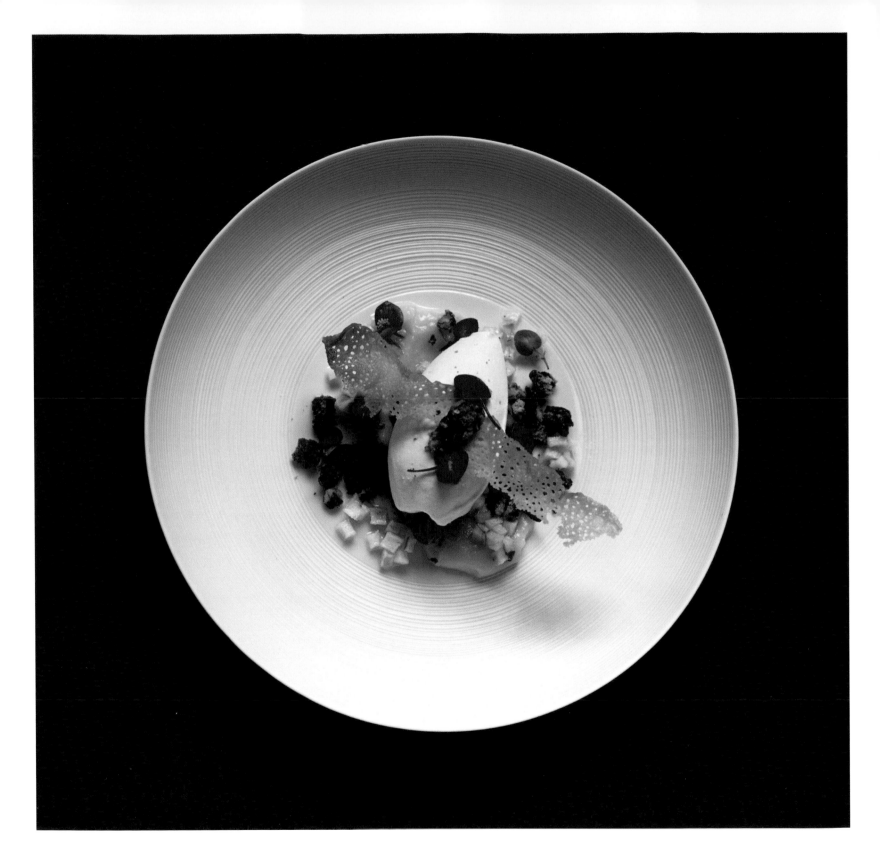

(continued from page 133)

crab apple compote

Place all the ingredients except the crab apples in a saucepan and bring to the boil, stirring to dissolve the sugar. Simmer for 3–4 minutes. Finely dice the crab apples, then immediately add them to the boiling syrup and remove the pan from the heat. Leave to cool. The syrup should retain enough heat to cook the diced apples perfectly, but do check them before the syrup is completely cold to make sure they are not over cooked; they should retain a little crispness. If they are not ready by the time the syrup has cooled down, return the pan to the heat briefly and remove the apples with a slotted spoon as soon as they are done. Return them to the syrup once it is cold.

serving

Place a spoonful of crab apple purée in the middle of each serving plate and spread it out a little. Sprinkle a line of the crumble mix on the plate at a diagonal. Drain the apple compote through a sieve and place a few small piles of apple around the plate. Scatter the apple blossom around and then place a large scoop of ice cream in the middle of the plate. Top with a little more crumble and an apple tuile. Finally, drizzle with some of the crab apple cooking juices.

petits fours

Petits fours are the last thing a customer eats before leaving the restaurant, so it is important to make sure they are just as memorable as the rest of the meal. There are so many different things you can do; as long as a little logic is applied to flavourings, anything goes.

When making a new petit four or chocolate, I think about the coffee – which, after all, they are served to accompany. Coffee has many different flavour notes: caramel, chocolate, liquorice, cardamom, nutmeg and chicory, to name but a few. So anything with these underlying flavours should work well. We serve between 12 and 16 petits fours at the restaurant, changing them now and again. The six in this chapter are some of my favourites.

lime leaf chocolate truffles

Although these are made with my standard rich truffle base, the highly aromatic lime leaves give the illusion of a lighter-tasting truffle. Lemongrass or rose geranium could be used instead. Pick a flavour you love and experiment with it.

juice and grated zest of 2 lemons
15 lime leaves, roughly shredded
325ml double cream
65g unsalted butter, diced
500g bitter chocolate (64–71 per cent
  cocoa solids), chopped
50ml Cointreau
cocoa powder for dusting

Place the lemon juice and zest in a saucepan with the lime leaves and bring to the boil. Add the double cream, return to the boil, then remove from the heat and set aside to infuse for 2–3 hours.

Pass the mixture through a fine sieve into a pan, pushing as much of the liquid through as possible. Bring to the boil and whisk in the diced butter a little at a time, then remove from the heat. Put the chopped chocolate in a bowl and pour in the hot cream. Stir until the chocolate has melted, then add the Cointreau. Place the mixture in the fridge for about 30 minutes to set just a little, then beat with an electric mixer for half a minute or so, until smooth and pliable.

Pipe into cone shapes on a baking tray lined with baking parchment (alternatively you could pipe it out in a long sausage shape and cut it across, or even just put teaspoonfuls of it on the baking parchment). Return to the fridge to set, then dust with cocoa powder. Store in the fridge.

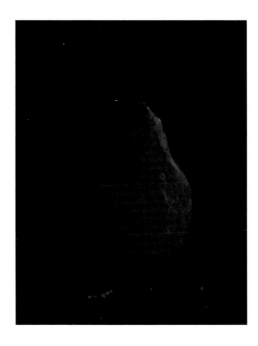

bitter chocolate fudge

This recipe appears in my first book, *Essence* (Absolute Press, 2006), but I have included it again here, with the addition of a little aniseed, because it is such a favourite with my customers – and with my wife, Helen. It makes a lovely accompaniment to strong espresso, especially if you use a coffee that has liquorice or aniseed notes.

You can omit the pistachios and raisins if you wish, or add some grated lemon or orange zest. You could try a chocolate with a different cocoa solids content, say 71 or 75 per cent, or omit the chocolate altogether and just make plain fudge flavoured with a little sea salt.

250ml liquid glucose
250g Demerara sugar
400ml double cream
250g bitter chocolate (64 per cent cocoa solids)
75g pistachios
75g raisins
50g green aniseed

Put the glucose, Demerara sugar and double cream in a large, heavy-based saucepan. Place on a moderate heat and bring slowly to the boil. Meanwhile, finely chop the chocolate. Sprinkle the chocolate into the boiling cream mixture, stirring until it dissolves. Turn the heat up and boil without stirring until it reaches 243°F on a sugar thermometer (this measure must be accurate, hence this specific Fahrenheit reading – centigrade isn't precise enough). Pour the mixture into the bowl of a food mixer and beat at medium speed until it has cooled a little.

Add the nuts, raisins and aniseed and beat one last time. Pour into a baking tray lined with baking parchment, cover and leave in the fridge to set. Cut into the desired shapes and store in an airtight container until needed.

white chocolate and salted lemon fudge

One of my sous chefs, Gary Pearce, came up with the initial idea for this recipe. It was very rich and a little soft, so together we worked on improving it. We needed some acidity to help balance the richness, so I suggested salted lemon, which goes fantastically well with the white chocolate.

That problem solved, we then set about making it a little harder. This was achieved by cutting down the amount of cream and taking the cooking of the fudge to a higher temperature. Now it's perfect. Job done!

300ml double cream
750g granulated sugar
250ml liquid glucose
400g white chocolate, chopped
50g unsalted butter, diced
125g Salted Lemons (see page 18), finely
*   chopped*

Put the double cream, granulated sugar and glucose in a large, heavy-based saucepan and bring slowly to the boil, stirring to dissolve the sugar. Raise the heat and boil until it reaches 130°C on a sugar thermometer, stirring frequently to prevent it catching on the bottom of the pan.

Transfer the mixture to the bowl of a freestanding food mixer and start beating on low speed. Add the chopped chocolate in 3 stages, allowing each one to be incorporated before adding the next. Then add the butter and beat well on low speed. Finally mix in the salted lemons.

Pour the mixture into a baking tray lined with baking parchment, place another sheet of parchment on top and leave to cool. Put it in the fridge to set. Cut it into the desired shapes and store in an airtight container until needed.

You could also pour some melted white chocolate on the fudge before cutting it, as in the picture.

blackcurrant and liquorice jelly

No collection of petits fours is complete without a jelly. It adds a pleasing contrast, a tang in the mouth. You can make all sorts of different flavours. Why not try star anise instead of liquorice? Cherry and verbena work well together, as do blood orange and coriander or, for something a little more unusual, carrot and cardamom.

500ml blackcurrant purée
3g ground liquorice root
150ml liquid glucose
500g caster sugar
35g pectin powder
15ml lemon juice

for dusting
100g caster sugar, mixed with
   75g granulated sugar

Place the blackcurrant purée, liquorice root, glucose and 400g of the caster sugar in a large saucepan and bring to the boil, stirring all the time. Boil until it reaches 102°C on a sugar thermometer, stirring occasionally so it doesn't catch on the bottom of the pan.

Mix the pectin powder with the remaining caster sugar. When the blackcurrant mixture reaches the correct temperature, add the pectin and sugar and whisk until dissolved, being careful as it will be extremely hot. Keep on a high heat and cook until it reaches 108°C, stirring occasionally. Whisk in the lemon juice and pass the mixture through a medium sieve into a baking tray lined with baking parchment, in a layer 1cm thick. Leave to cool, then place in the fridge to set. Cut into the desired shapes and dust them with the sugar (you could add a little citric acid powder to the sugar mix to give them a sour coating).

chicory macaroons

These little macaroons make a great accompaniment to coffee. They include chocolate, caramel and chicory flavour notes – all of which can also be found in good coffee.

To make chocolate macaroons, substitute cocoa powder for the chicory. You could also try a different filling – coffee cream and burdock cream would both be great.

Makes 18

for the chicory macaroons
200g caster sugar
50ml water
140g egg whites (4–5 whites)
200g icing sugar
200g ground almonds
30ml chicory essence

for the chicory ganache
70ml double cream
10ml chicory essence
100g bitter chocolate (71 per cent cocoa solids), chopped
30g unsalted butter

chicory macaroons
Put the caster sugar and water in a heavy-based pan and heat gently, stirring to dissolve the sugar. Raise the heat, bring to the boil and cook without stirring until the syrup reaches 120°C on a sugar thermometer. When it reaches approximately 110°C, whisk the egg whites to soft peaks in a freestanding electric mixer. When the syrup reaches the correct temperature, slowly pour it on to the whites, whisking constantly. Carry on whisking until the mixture is thick and very stiff.

Mix the icing sugar and ground almonds together and add slowly to the egg whites, gently folding them in. Finally fold in the chicory essence. Place in a piping bag and pipe on to a tray lined with baking parchment, making rounds approximately 3cm in diameter. Allow to dry for about 30 minutes. This is important, as it allows a skin to form before you bake them. Place in an oven preheated to 180°C/Gas Mark 4 and bake for 8–12 minutes. Ideally the vent of the oven should be open, but you could just prop the door open slightly. The macaroons should be firm to the touch and crisp when cool. Remove from the oven, leave to cool, and then remove from the baking parchment.

chicory ganache
Put the double cream and chicory essence in a small saucepan and bring to the boil. Remove from the heat and put to one side for 2 minutes. Put the chopped chocolate in a bowl and pour on the hot cream. Stir until the chocolate has melted, then add the butter and stir until amalgamated. Leave to cool completely, then whisk until smooth. Sandwich the macaroons together with the ganache.

savarins

The saying goes that you should be able to drink a savarin, and these wonderful little yeast cakes are moist, light and alcoholic. They are quite time consuming to make but well worth the effort. If you prefer, you could make larger ones to serve for afternoon tea.

Chopped figs or apricots could be substituted for the raisins. If you would like to change the flavourings in the soaking syrup, try spices, smoked tea, coffee or, for a more acidic approach, fresh pineapple juice – in which case the glaze could be a passion fruit one.

Makes 30–40

for the savarins
75g unsalted butter
10g fresh yeast
75ml warm water
25ml double cream
25g caster sugar
200g strong white flour
5g salt
2$^{1}/_{2}$ eggs
seeds from 1 vanilla pod
grated zest of $^{1}/_{2}$ lemon
grated zest of $^{1}/_{2}$ orange
50g raisins, chopped

for the syrup
1 vanilla pod
500ml water
200g golden caster sugar
50ml rum (or other spirit)
4 strips of orange zest

for the glaze
150g apricot jam
75ml water

savarins

Place the butter in a frying pan over a medium heat and cook until golden brown. Cool quickly and then pour through a fine sieve into a bowl. Set aside.

Whisk the yeast with the water and cream, then add the sugar and 50g of the flour and whisk well. Leave in a warm place for 15 minutes.

Place the remaining flour in the bowl of a freestanding electric mixer with the yeast mixture and all the other ingredients except the butter and raisins. Beat for 5 minutes on a low speed, then slowly add the butter and beat for 2 minutes. Mix in the raisins. Divide the mixture between 30–40 buttered savarin moulds, 2.5cm in diameter, and leave in a warm place for about 30 minutes, until doubled in size. Meanwhile, make the syrup and the glaze (below).

Place the savarins in an oven preheated to 180°C/Gas Mark 4 and bake for 7–8 minutes, until golden brown. Remove from the oven and leave to cool for 4 minutes, then turn

them out of the moulds. While they are still warm, add them to the pan of the syrup and leave to soak for about 4 minutes, until plumped up. Take out of the syrup, squeezing the savarins lightly to remove the excess. Roll them in the glaze until evenly coated, then place in petits fours cases and insert a little toothpick in the top of each one.

syrup

Slit the vanilla pod open lengthwise, scrape out the seeds and cut the pod into small pieces. Put the seeds and pod in a pan with all the remaining ingredients and bring to the boil, stirring to dissolve the sugar. Simmer for 5 minutes, then remove from the heat and cool to blood temperature.

glaze

Put the jam and water in a small saucepan and bring to the boil, whisking occasionally. Remove from the heat and pass through a fine sieve. Place back on the heat and cook for 5 minutes, until it is the consistency of a thick syrup. Remove from the heat and keep warm.

glossary

Below is a brief guide to the wild foods I use in desserts, plus some of the more unusual ingredients in this book. Many of them are available from the suppliers listed on page 148.

acorns

We pick acorns on our autumn walks in the woods. When roasted (see Acorn Tiramisu, page 131), they have a deep, magical taste of spices, chocolate, coffee and caramel.

agar agar

This is derived from red dulse, a form of seaweed, and is a good setting agent. I use it in jellies, such as the Muscovado and Rum Jelly on page 61; it also allows you to make warm mousses, as it doesn't start to melt until approximately 83°C. It is available in most healthfood shops.

angelica
(*angelica sylvestris*)

We are lucky enough to have angelica growing in our back yard, so it gets put to good use. It is part of the lovage family and is sometimes known as black lovage. The taste is very green, with a hint of citrus and a little juniper, and thus complements dishes containing citrus.

burdock
(*arctium lappa*)

A wonderful plant that you can use in its entirety - seeds, leaves, roots, stalks and all. It can be found on roadsides, in waste places and on most country walks.
The root has a deep, warming taste and is relatively easily available dried, which is a good job because it is a real pain to dig up. The Japanese serve the fresh root as a vegetable.

carrageen moss
(*chondrus crispus*)

A form of red algae, this setting agent is available dried or powdered. You should be able to find it in healthfood shops.

cassia bark

Also known as Chinese cinnamon, this has a slightly less aggressive and somewhat deeper flavour than ordinary cinnamon.

cobnuts
(*corylus avellana*)

The fruits of the wild hazelnut tree are quite common in woods and hedges all around Britain. They are ready for harvesting from late August till November, depending on the weather. You will have to rush to gather them though, as the squirrels will probably beat you.

crab apples
(*malus sylvestris*)

You can find crab apples in hedgerows, woods and some gardens. They are traditionally used for jellies and to make a sour juice, but we use them for mousses, compotes, parfaits and in a crumble (see page 133).

elderberries
(*sambucus nigra*)

First we have the elderflower and then come the clusters of dark-purple elderberries, fruiting from mid August to September. Their deep, rich, fruity flavour makes them ideal for sorbets, mousses, in an apple pie or even in a chilled red wine and elderberry soup.

elderflowers
(*sambucus nigra*)

Very common both in the countryside and in towns, elderflowers have a brief season from May to June. They have the most fantastic fragrance, which enhances so many desserts - in particular ones containing gooseberries and rhubarb.

galangal

Used throughout Southeast Asia, this is related to the ginger family but has a mellower flavour, with a light citrus note. Fresh ginger can be substituted if necessary.

gorse flowers
(*ulex europaeus*)

Gorse bushes grow on heaths and dry, sandy hills. They start to flower in May but are at their best in June and July. Their wonderful scent is reminiscent of coconut and banana. Be careful when you pick them, as they are surrounded by very sharp thorns. To dry gorse flowers, see page 116.

green aniseed

This is one of my favourite spices. I love aniseed drinks, such as pastis, ouzo and raki, and have paired it with chocolate on many occasions. It is traditionally used in cakes and pastries in the Mediterranean and is also very good for the digestion.

Clockwise from left: angelica leaf; carrageen moss; burdock root

145 *dessert*   glossary

Clockwise from top-left: dried hibiscus flowers; mastic resin; pandan leaf; salep

grue de cacao

Grue de cacao consists of cocoa beans that have been cleaned, roasted and lightly crushed. Both bitter and sweet at the same time, the taste is slightly nutty, with a hint of alcohol. Grue is very crisp, making it ideal for a garnish when you need to add texture. Available from specialist chocolate shops.

hibiscus

Hibiscus flowers have a lovely deep burgundy colour. They add sourness and a slight redcurrant flavour to desserts. You should be able to find dried hibiscus in Caribbean shops and some healthfood shops.

lemon verbena

Brought to Europe by the Spanish in the eighteenth century, this has the most amazing lemon sherbet flavour. It grows in our yard, and when we brush past it in summer the scent is glorious. It makes delicious ice creams and is a useful flavouring for fruit compotes. Although not easy to find in shops, it is well worth cultivating in your garden, as it grows like wildfire.

mastic

Related to the pistachio tree, this is native to Greece and Turkey. It is grown for its resin, which is dried in tiny boulders. The unique flavour goes well with citrus and pineapple.

meadowsweet

(filipendula ulmaria/spiraea ulmaria)
Meadowsweet can be found in damp woods, fields and marshy areas. It flowers from early May until October in warm summers, and the sweet-scented blossoms are ideal for infusing in cream to make ice creams, parfaits and syllabubs.

pandan leaf

Belonging to the screwpine family, pandan leaves are used all over Southeast Asia. They are even sometimes made into a little basket in which to steam rice. I love the nutty, toasted-rice flavour of the leaves in moderation, but I find if too much is used they can taste almost fishy. They are wonderful in ice creams, brûlées, rice pudding and tapioca and go very well with pineapple and mango.

rowanberries

(sorbus aucuparia)
The orangey-red fruits of the rowan tree, also known as the mountain ash, start to ripen in the middle of August but are at their best at the end of September. Their flavour is almost like marmalade. Rowanberries are traditionally turned into jams and jellies but I think they deserve to be used much more creatively than this.

salep

Salep is the dried and powdered root of several species of orchid. Used as a thickener, it has a unique flavour. I first came across it in Turkey, where it is often added to ice cream.

sheep's sorrel

(rumex acetosella)
These wonderful, arrowhead-shaped leaves grow in fields and pastures. As with all sorrels, they have a pleasing lemony bite and make a great ice cream (see page 119).

sumac

These very sour seeds come from certain varieties of the sumac tree and are used mostly in the Middle East, where they tend to grow wild. They can be soaked in water, then pounded and used instead of lemon juice.

violet

(viola odorata)
The sweet violet has a haunting, exceptionally floral flavour. It partners red fruits, peaches and apricots extremely well and is also good with citrus fruit. If you buy them, make sure you choose unsprayed ones; do not use African violets, as they are not edible.

wood sorrel

(oxalis acetosella)
Also known as oxalis, wood sorrel grows from March onwards in damp areas and ancient woods, especially pinewoods. Its lemony tang makes it a suitable garnish for desserts.

my suppliers

g. baldwin and co.

171–3 Walworth Road
London SE17 1RW
0207 703 5550
www.baldwins.co.uk

Suppliers of a huge range of dried herbs, roots and flowers, including burdock root.

devon violet nursery

Meadow View
Hayne Lane
Honiton
Devon EX14 3PD
01404 813701
www.sweetviolets.co.uk

Specialises in rare varieties of sweet violet.

the mountain food company ltd

Banc-y-ddol
Hebron
Whitland
Dyfed
01994 419555
www.mountainfood.org

The immensely knowledgeable Yun Hider supplies wild foods such as sorrel, gorse flowers and meadowsweet – invaluable when I am too busy to get out, and for wild foods from the sea.

msk

PO Box 1592
Dronfield
Sheffield S18 8BR
01246 412211
www.msk-ingredients.com

MSK supplies us with some of the gums, agar and pralines that we use, and has all the ingredients the modern chef needs. Have a good look at the website; it's very interesting.

sambava spices

Unit 2, Roseberry Place
Bath BA2 3DU
01225 426309
www.sambavaspices.com

I get some of my more unusual spices from James Ransome, such as wattleseed and mastic.

equipment

bodo sperlein ltd

Unit 1.05, OXO Tower
Barge House Street
London SE1 9PH
020 7633 9413
www.bodosperlein.com

A big thank you to Bodo again for supplying us with some of the most interesting china used in this book. Wonderful shapes and lines.

cheltenham kitchener

4 Queens Circus
Cheltenham GL50 1RX
01242 235688
www.kitchenercookware.com

It's great to have this equipment supplier just around the corner. If Ed can't get it, I don't know who can.

magrini ltd

Unit 5, Maybrook Industrial Estate
Brownhills
Walsall
West Midlands WS8 7DG
01543 375311
www.cookingconcepts.co.uk

A wonderful company with all those big, cheffy pieces of equipment at the cutting edge of cooking, and a few smaller ones too. Graham Bagnall is a font of knowledge about all his equipment. Well worth a look.

Salep root and powdered salep (see page 147).

index

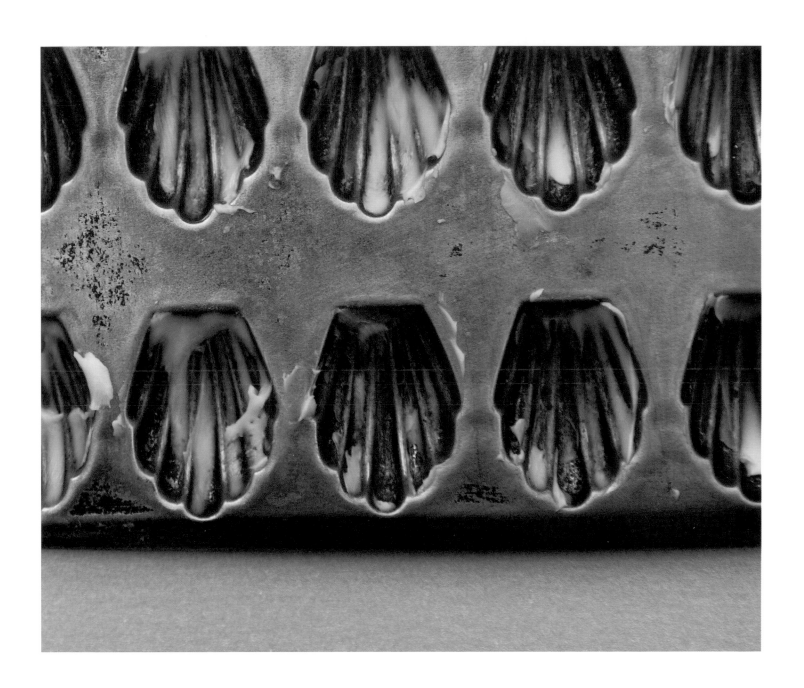

acknowledgements

With thanks to my team in the kitchen: to
Gary, my second chef and a major prop for
me to run my ideas by; and to Adam and
Ciaran for their hard work and boundless
enthusiasm. Thank you for your effort,
patience and inspiration.

A special thanks to my panel of tasters
(the girls out front): Helen, Justyna, and
Stephanie. Thank you for your comments
and your insatiable appetite for desserts.
I sometimes think we can't make them
fast enough!

Thanks once again to Lisa Barber for
being my photographer on this project.
The brilliance of her work speaks for itself.
And last but not least, thanks to my
publisher, Absolute Press. Jon and Meg,
thank you for approaching me to do a
second book; the first can't have been
too bad. Thanks to Matt and Claire, for
making the design as good as the first
book. Thanks to Jane Middleton, for
bearing with me and helping with the
finishing touches.

The biggest thank you goes to our
customers, for their continued support
both in the restaurant and in book sales.

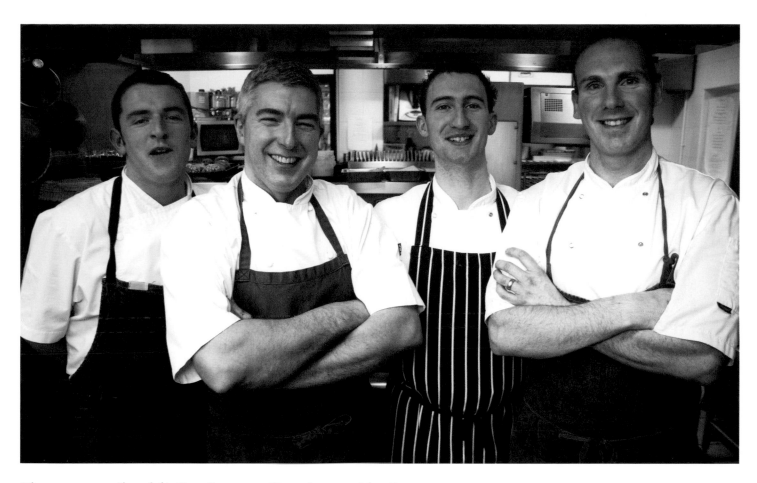

The current team (from left): Gary Pearce, me, Ciaran Sweeney, Adam Brown